Walking for the Health of It

The Easy and Effective Exercise for People Over 50

Jeannie Ralston

An AARP Book
published by
American Association of Retired Persons
Washington, D.C.
Scott, Foresman and Company
Lifelong Learning Division
Glenview, Illinois

Copyright © 1986 by Jeannie Ralston
All Rights Reserved
Printed in the United States of America
123456-KPF-919089888786

Suggested Walking Exercise Program on page 33 from *The Aerobics Program for Total Well-Being* by Dr. Kenneth H. Cooper. Copyright © 1982 by Kenneth H. Cooper. Adapted by permission of the publisher, M. Evans and Co., Inc., New York, NY 10017.

Stride Cycle on page 36 from *Human Walking* by Verne T. Inman, et al. Copyright © 1981 Williams & Wilkins Co., Baltimore. Adapted by permission of the publisher and Dr. H. J. Ralston.

Weight tables on page 93 courtesy of Statistical Bulletin, Metropolitan Life Insurance Company.

Library of Congress Cataloging-in-Publication Data

Ralston, Jeannie.
    Walking for the health of it.

    Includes bibliographical references and index.
    1. Walking.   2. Exercise for the aged.   I. Title.
RA781.65.R35   1986   613.7´1´0880565   86-3910

ISBN 0-673-24826-7

AARP Books is an educational and public service project of the American Association of Retired Persons, which, with a membership of more than 21 million, is the largest association of persons fifty and over in the world today. Founded in 1958, AARP provides older Americans with a wide range of membership programs and services, including legislative representation at both federal and state levels. For further information about additional association activities, write to AARP, 1909 K Street, N.W., Washington, DC 20049.

To my parents, Jack and Jeannette, with much love.

Contents

Acknowledgments

I would like to thank first and foremost Scott Fallon for his research, his ideas, and his unfailing support. Thanks also to Agnes Birnbaum for her role in making this project happen; to Franklin Ashley for his inspiration; and to Jane Pratt, Andrew Postman, Mary Beth D'Amico, and Julie Jameson for their help.

(1)

Why Walk?

You are flipping through a magazine when you come across an ad that shows a man with a body Charles Atlas would envy sitting on a weight-lifting contraption. "No Pain, No Gain," the headline reads. You shake your head and turn the page.

You're watching television one Saturday afternoon, all cozy and comfortable in your lounge chair, when a sports program comes on. The main feature that day is a triathlon—hundreds of people swimming, bicycling, and running miles and miles all in one day, some to the point of exhaustion. "They're crazy," you say as you sink farther back in your chair.

You have to go to the supermarket, so you jump into the car and start driving the one mile. On the way, you pass two joggers, both soaked in sweat with their lower jaws hanging open, gasping for breath. You roll down the window to let in some air.

OK. So you know there's a fitness fad going on. There's no way you can escape the fact. Everywhere around you are athletes—weekend ones and otherwise—stretching, sweating, and straining; reports about how exercise can improve your health and make you feel better; high fashions inspired by exercise clothes; social networks built around exercise; and friends and relatives who talk of little else but the topspin on a tennis serve, the birdie just missed on the eighth hole, or the number of miles covered on a bicycle.

If none of this has spurred you to action, you are not alone. According to a recent Harris poll, 63 percent of the American public—and 70 percent of Americans over fifty years old—lead sedentary lives, opting for sports where all they have to do is spectate, for air-conditioning over aerobic conditioning, and for stretching out in a hammock over stretching their hamstrings. It has little to do with laziness—it's just that they have never thought exercise could add anything to their lives and that they view exercise as being difficult, taxing, *uncomfortable*. Slogans like "No pain, no gain" only reinforce this attitude. Most people who aren't exercising think that they have to be born athletes to participate, that they can't just *start* exercising after years of doing nothing, and that exercise is something for young people with seemingly infinite reserves of energy.

Well, good news. There's an activity you *have* done most of your life—no matter how sedentary you are—that can be turned into an exercise that doesn't hurt, that's simple to do, and that can give you all the benefits of those "hard" exercises. It's walking. Yes, that same activity you learned to do when you were about a year old can help get you in shape, no matter what age you are now.

How can something so easy and natural be good for you? You may be thinking that you have to walk on your hands or pull a U-Haul trailer or walk fifty miles in half a day to get some real benefit out of walking. But I'm talking about upright walking, unencumbered, at reasonable distances and speeds. You'll need to walk faster than the pace you use when you're window-shopping or strolling at the zoo, but by slowly working up to a brisker speed—about three to four miles per hour—it won't be uncomfortable.

The Exercise of the Eighties

Some exercise experts are calling walking "the exercise of the eighties." That's a pretty lofty phrase for an activity that not long ago wasn't considered "real exercise" by many fitness fans because it was so easy. But now that some joggers and doctors are running out of enthusiasm for running because of the high risk of injury, walking has attracted a growing following and some glowing words. "Walking is the best exercise there is. It uses more of the body's muscles than many other types of exercises, improves cardiovascular efficiency, and is virtually injury-free," reports Dr. Ronald Lawrence, a former medical advisor to the U.S. Olympic Committee and the President's Council on Physical Fitness and Sports.

Dr. Kenneth H. Cooper, author of *The Aerobics Program for Total Well-Being* and popularizer of the principles of aerobic conditioning (a system of conditioning that improves respiratory and circulatory function through exercises that increase the consumption of oxygen), rates walking as one of the five major aerobic exercises. "The great advantage of walking is that it can be done anywhere by anyone, regardless of age or sex," he says.

Even an ardent antiexerciser such as Dr. Henry A. Solomon, a New York cardiologist and author of *The Exercise Myth*, cannot deny the value of walking. Just as all sedentary people were starting to feel smug about his "Down with the fitness boom" theories, Solomon concluded in his book, "The ideal exercise in virtually every respect is walking. Certainly nothing could be more convenient. . . . It is just about the safest activity you could think of."

Lest you think, though, that this emphasis on and excitement about the oldest form of human transportation is just a passing fad, note what Thomas Jefferson said two centuries ago: "Of all exercises, walking is the best." And consider this from Hippocrates back in ancient Greece: "Walking is man's best medicine."

Some 50 million Americans have seen the wisdom of the experts' words and have taken to the sidewalks, the paths, and the streets in their walking shoes—people, just like you and me, who didn't think they could ever stick to a fitness program or who stopped doing other exercises, such as running and aerobic dancing, that were too strenuous. Walking has the lowest dropout rate of any form of exercise and is the only exercise in which the rate of participation does not decline in the middle and later years. A recent survey released by the President's Council on Physical Fitness and Sports found that the largest group of regular walkers—39.4 percent—were men sixty-five years and older.

"Before I started walking a few years ago, I used to play tennis every morning with some other women. Now I walk two miles five days a week, and I like it much better. I don't have to think as much when I walk," reports Peet Adams, fifty-six, of Kingsport, Tennessee.

"I used to be terribly sedentary," says Jo Harper, a sixty-three-year-old Colorado walker. "I always thought I was too old to exercise. Finally, I got on my feet and started jogging, but I developed shinsplints and tendonitis, so I began walking." That was three years ago. Today this fan of footwork walks twice a day—once in the morning for two miles, and again in the evening with her husband for two miles—and hardly ever misses because walking makes her feel "fabulous."

Why So Popular?

People turn to walking over other exercises, especially running, for several reasons. First, it's much easier on your body. Each time a jogger takes a step, three to four times the body weight beats down on the feet, which often causes shinsplints and tendonitis. Brisk walking, on the other hand, only puts one and a half times the body weight on the feet. Also, many runners have tight, overdeveloped muscles in the backs of their legs without comparable development in the front, according to Howard Jacobson, an Olympic racewalking coach. When one muscle group is excessively stronger than its opposing group, the chances of injury in the weaker group are greatly increased, he says. Dr. George Sheehan, the well-known "guru" of running, maintains that a runner who regularly averages fifty miles a week has a 73 percent chance of eventually incurring an injury that will force him or her to stop running for a considerable amount of time.

Walkers, though, are rarely injured because walking

actually has a massaging effect on muscles. There's a greater stability to the walking motion because one foot is always on the ground and the transfer of weight from one foot to the other is smoother. This means less risk of twisting and hurting your legs. Nevertheless, walking uses up almost as many calories as those more strenuous exercises. According to the President's Council on Physical Fitness and Sports, a recent test of energy expended by twenty-four healthy males during walks, jogs, and runs of varying speeds showed that jogging a mile in 8 1/2 minutes burns only twenty-six calories more than walking a mile in 12 minutes.

Another reason people like walking is that it's cheap. Exercise suits, rackets, or expensive equipment isn't required—all you really need is a good pair of walking shoes. Moreover, if you use walking to replace short car trips, you can pocket the money you save on gas.

One thing I personally enjoy about walking is its spontaneity. With how many other sports can you just go and *do* when the mood hits or when you have some unexpected free time? You don't have to call to make court reservations or find a friend to play with or allot extra time for a change of clothes or a shower. You don't have to devote several hours to walking if you don't want to, as you do if you play a set of tennis or a round of golf. Besides, you can make it a pleasant social activity. It is a perfect opportunity to catch up on the latest news with a friend or to spend private time with your spouse or another family member.

Walking is perfect for people who have never exercised because it doesn't require lessons and because you will not be conspicuous as a beginner. Even if your heart is set on running or cycling but you haven't exercised in years, you should start your exercise program by walking. It is an ideal stepping-stone to more strenuous sports. It will get you in shape, get you familiar with your body and its capabilities, and get you used to sticking to a regular program. It will also give you confidence.

But the main reason for being on a walking program is that it will improve your health and fitness. This point can't be stressed enough. Walking will help make your heart more efficient; improve your circulation and the efficiency of your lungs; help you lose weight, sleep better, and relieve stress; and help you deal with certain types of arthritis and osteoporosis. These are just a few of the medical benefits. If more Americans get fit, it is likely that a big chunk will be taken out of the $175 billion spent annually on medical bills.

Even though there is no definitive evidence that exercise increases longevity, several studies suggest that this is so, including the Framingham Study, a landmark research project that has followed the health habits of the citizens of a Massachusetts town for forty years. Dr. William. B. Kannel and Dr. Paul Sorlie report that "epidemiologic studies have generally shown the protective effect of physically active occupations and [regular] leisure exercise. Lack of exercise appears to shorten life span and predispose the individual to lethal heart attacks." Many life insurance companies, including Allstate and the ITT Life Insurance Corporation, are so confident that physical activity leads to longer life that they are giving people who regularly exercise discounts on their policies.

"Exercise is the closest thing to an antiaging pill now available. It is not that old men sit around most of the time. It is that sitting around ages men before their time," according to gerontologist Dr. Josef P. Hrachovec. Thomas Cureton, an exercise physiologist, adds a corollary: "The human body is the only machine that breaks down when *not* used. Moreover, it's also the only mechanism that functions better the more it is put to use." And Dr. Everett L. Smith, of the Department of Preventive Medicine at the University of Wisconsin, estimates that 50 percent of the decline in biological functions between the ages of thirty and seventy is due to disuse.

The American Medical Association, too, has recognized that exercise is one of the best preventive medicines and that the real key to total wellness lies within the individual—not the health care community. "You must learn to accept the fact that your health is primarily in your hands. What you do to your body—and for your body—is the largest determinant of whether you will need medical care," the AMA stated in a recent report.

A Positive Approach

While a healthier life is what walking can bring you, walking shouldn't be viewed only as a means to an end. The most successful fitness programs are those in which an exerciser enjoys the activity as well as the results. If you go into a walking program thinking, "This is something I have to do," or, "Everyone else is exercising, so I guess I will too," you're not likely to stick with it. A positive attitude is all-important; you should walk for the sheer pleasure of it, for fun and self-fulfillment. "A man's exercise must be play," says Dr. George Sheehan, "or it will do him little good." And that goes for women too.

I walk to and from work every day in Manhattan. I could easily take a bus or the subway—it would be much faster. But I never have because the time I walk is the time I use to warm up for work and then to wind down from it. No one makes me do it. I do it because I like to witness New York waking up and then see it sparkling with glamour as evening approaches and because no matter what goes wrong during the day, I know I've at least done one good thing for myself. Once you start a walking program, you'll find your own reasons to love it. The results, when you start to see them, will seem to have come almost effortlessly.

Now is the time to get started, to get moving. Dispel the myth that you can be too old to exercise. Now is much, much better than never. If you never exercise, you may never know the joy, the satisfaction, and the comfort of good health.

Stop! If someone asked you to start exercising today, your response would be _____ . Now turn the page.

Does your response sound similar to any of these?

15 Common Excuses for Not Exercising

1. I don't have the time.
2. I don't like to sweat.
3. I'm afraid I'll hurt myself.
4. It's boring.
5. The weather's bad.
6. Exercise equipment costs too much.
7. I'm too tired as it is. I don't want to expend the energy.
8. I don't know how to do it right. There's no one around to teach me how to do it, and I can't afford lessons.
9. I don't have anyone to do it with.
10. The gym or pool or courts are too crowded.
11. I have too much pressure from work to think about exercise.
12. My daily routine varies so much that it would be impossible to stick to a program.
13. I just don't think I could stay with it.
14. I haven't exercised in twenty-five years, and I feel fine.
15. I'm too old.

You don't get off that easy. Each excuse can be debunked.

15 Reasons You Should Be Walking.

1. You can fit walking into your schedule easier than any other exercise. You don't have to allot time for a clothes change, a shower, or getting to the gym, and you can accomplish other tasks, such as shopping, while you walk.
2. Even though walking will raise your heartbeat and can condition you aerobically, it will rarely make you perspire so much that you will have to change your clothes.
3. Walking can give you the benefits of more strenuous exercise without any of the risks of serious injuries.
4. If you think walking is boring, you've never used it to clear your mind of the day's tensions, to think about the day's events, to soak up the scenery, or to talk to a loved one *alone*. Besides, nowadays you can take along entertainment in a personal stereo with headphones. What could be better than stepping out to Tchaikovsky?
5. Walking is a year-round sport. If you follow the advice in chapter 12, you can walk in the heat, the rain, the cold, and the dark. The intensity is mild enough to make walking perfect for any weather.
6. The only basic equipment you need for walking is a good pair of walking shoes.
7. You'll find that walking (or any exercise) will actually give you *more* energy. You'll get your blood moving, and your lungs filled with fresh air, and you'll feel refreshed physically and mentally.
8. You learned how to do it when you were a baby, so you can hardly help but do it right.
9. You don't need a partner in walking, as in tennis or racquetball, but having one often makes walking nicer.

10. The streets, woods, and fields are never too crowded for walking.
11. Walking can actually help reduce life's pressures. Better circulation, increased oxygen intake, and increased muscle activity have a relaxing effect on the body.
12. Your walking program can fit easily into your daily routine. You can walk while doing errands, on your way to work, at lunch, on a coffee break, or after work. So many options!
13. Walking has the lowest dropout rate of any form of exercise. If you can make the commitment to stay with it for six to eight weeks, you're more than likely going to get hooked.
14. Even if you think you're perfectly healthy without exercising, walking is a safeguard that can help ward off diseases and maladies that could affect you in your later years.
15. Walking is one of the few exercises that almost anyone of any age can do safely, easily, and enjoyably.

(2)

Getting Your Feet out the Door

Where do you begin? Do you just slide into your sneakers, step outside, and start walking? Does that mean you are on an exercise program? You could, of course, do just that, but it really wouldn't do you much good in the long run. If you go about it in that haphazard way, you will be lucky if you stick with your walking for a week. What you need to do before you step out the door is put structure into your program.

Without a plan, you might be uncomfortable because you wore the wrong shoes or even hurt yourself by doing too much too soon and decide to return to your sedentary lifestyle. Experts estimate that about half of those who start exercise programs drop out in the initial stages. How you go about starting your program can determine whether it will become a permanent pastime or a passing fancy and how much benefit you will get from it.

To get your program on the right track, begin by walking into your doctor's office for a complete physical examination and a stress test. If your doctor doesn't administer stress tests, he or she should be able to tell you where to get one. Many fitness experts recommend that anyone over thirty-five be checked by a doctor before he or she begins exercising. It is even more important if you are over fifty, especially if it has been years since you have exercised. In a stress test, a health professional will monitor, among other things, your heart and respiration rates while you exercise on a treadmill or stationary bicycle (the stress test will be explained further in chapter 3). When your doctor has the results of your physical examination and stress test, he or she will be able to suggest an exercise prescription for you and offer specific warnings about any health problems that might hinder your exercise activities.

Once you have the go-ahead to start your walking program, it is a good idea to record your vital statistics: blood pressure, resting heart rate, body measurements, and weight. This is not absolutely necessary, but it can serve as positive reinforcement later if you are able to see the progress you have made in terms of target heart rate or lost pounds or inches. One word of warning if you are going to do this: Do not check your progress every week or expect to see immediate changes. Unrealistically high expectations can lead to frustration and can cause you to give up when reality doesn't cooperate. Put your personal statistics away; pull them out after several months, but still do not be discouraged if you haven't taken four inches off your thighs. The changes in your body may come slowly, but rest assured that if you faithfully follow your walking program, they will come.

Getting Motivated

One of the most important elements of an exercise program is attitude. It is your body that is going to be doing the work, but it is your mind that is going to be spurring your body on. If you are not up for your program mentally, you are not going to be up for it physically either. Making the jump from a sedentary to a sportful lifestyle requires a good deal of dedication, motivation, and patience, and many people just don't think they have it in them to keep at it. But once you start, you will find that your program is fueled by pride—pride that you have the courage to do something to ebb the tide of aging, pride in your well-functioning body.

"When you get to be over fifty, it's the quality of life

that motivates you," says Bob Bernstein, fifty-four, who recently started walking with a New York City walking club. "I want to feel good every day, and I feel better than I did before I started walking. That's what motivates me."

But if you feel that you need even more motivation, you might want to write a contract with yourself to make your commitment formal. It should start out something like this: "As of this date, I, John Brown, am committing myself to walking three times a week for at least a half hour each day." Have your family witness the contract and then post it where it will be a constant reminder and source of encouragement to keep moving. You should include in the contract any goals you want to set for yourself, such as increasing your time to forty-five minutes after a few months. But again, it is important to keep your expectations realistic, or they may become a source of *dis*couragement. Also, put down any rewards you might want to give yourself for sticking to the program, such as treating yourself to a movie for every week you stay with it—at least for the first few months. While some people will include punishments for themselves if they fail to keep up the pace, such as having to do extra chores around the house, it is better to emphasize the positive. The loss of your reward is enough punishment, and you will have a much better time if you walk for rewards—both physical and psychological ones—rather than to avoid punishment.

"While behavior can be shaped by either reward or punishment, most psychologists find rewards to be more effective," says Dr. Roy J. Shephard, past president of the American College of Sports Medicine. Rewards are particularly important in the early stages of an exercise program because at this point participants may perceive some aspects of exercise negatively, such as fatigue, investment of time, and failure to realize goals. Shephard maintains that one of the big turning points in exercise motivation is when a person can move from dependence on any external rewards to the internal rewards of the exercise itself—feeling better and developing an attractive body.

Talk about your walking program to family, friends, and co-workers, and encourage them to ask about your progress. The more people who know about your commitment, the less likely you are to renege on it. You will not want to have to say, "Oh, I gave it up," when your boss inquires, "How's the walking going?" Also, it helps to keep a calendar posted in your home along with your contract. Each day that you walk, write down what time of day you went out, how far you went, and how long it took you.

When you start an exercise program, there is a tendency to think, "Ugh, I have to do this the rest of my life." Yes, exercise should be a lifelong commitment, but it can sometimes be overwhelming to think of it in that context at the outset. The secret is to get started one step at a time, literally. Concentrate only on doing your walking for that day. It helps to think positive thoughts during your walk or even speak them aloud to yourself. When you finish your walk, congratulate yourself; then you can start thinking about when you are going to fit in your next walk. This way an exercise program seems more manageable, and you will probably find that after a few months you won't have to use this method because your walking will have become a habit.

"I tell people if they can just stick with it for six to eight weeks, they'll be fine," says Kate Booth, director of the Morristown (New Jersey) Memorial Hospital Cardiac Rehabilitation Center. "They'll get into the rhythm of the exercise, and it'll be easier to stay with it."

The Buddy System

When it comes to sticking with an exercise regimen, you can get a little help from your friends. Nothing boosts motivation more than starting a walking program with someone else who will be waiting for you on those chilly mornings when it is so tempting to just sink under the covers for an extra forty-five minutes. When I first started walking to work, I did so with a friend who lived two blocks away, and there were many mornings when I might have preferred to jump on a subway had I not known we had a standing date to meet on my corner at 8:00 A.M. (She felt the same way.)

"I find that the companionship is crucial with walking," says Marie Saunders, fifty, a New York psychotherapist who joined the ranks of walkers because she didn't like jogging. "It's great having someone to talk to out there; it makes the walk go by so much faster. The woman I've been walking with has really become a good friend. When I jogged, I couldn't maintain a conversation with anyone."

Walking is an especially good exercise to do with your spouse, if you are married. It can provide peaceful time together or encourage conversation that you may not have time for during your busy days. "When my husband and I walk, it is a very nice time to be with each other," says Frances Ambrose, fifty, from Florham Park, New Jersey, who used walking as part of her recovery from a back operation. "Usually when we're home together, he's doing something and I'm doing something else. It's wonderful to get away together."

While it helps to discuss your progress with a walking buddy, be careful not to compare your results with your friend's or spouse's. You are not in competition with each other. You are both on the same team, striving for the same goal—bettering your lives. So be happy if your buddy loses a few pounds or lowers his or her heart rate, and work that much harder—with her or his help—to do the same.

Finding Time

OK, now you are all revved up to begin walking; you may even have found a friend who wants to do it with you. If you are going to get anywhere at all, you have to overcome another large hurdle that stands in the way of a successful walking program—finding the time. "No time" is the most common reason exercise programs crumble. Yes, you want to exercise, but there is a report due at work or your hair appointment or your weekly bridge game, or maybe the movie you have long wanted to see is on television. It is vital that you make walking one of your top priorities, or you will always be finding something else that you've "just got to do" instead.

When it comes to scheduling your exercise, you will be glad that you chose walking as your activity. It can fit into your schedule more unobtrusively than other exercises. Some people—like Ann Fields, a sixty-four-year-old Virginian—find it easier to walk in the morning. "I sneak out before anybody else in the house wakes up. A nice walk is a refreshing way to start the day. I get my exercise out of the way, so I feel proud of myself the rest of the day," says Ann. Or maybe you are like Andrew Grimes, fifty-eight, a hospital consultant from Nashville, Tennessee: "I usually walk at about four or five in the afternoon. I've tried walking in the morning, but I just can't get my hinges moving that early." (If you do save walking until the last part of the day, though, make sure it does not become your last priority as well.)

When you walk depends on whether you are a day or night person and, of course, on your schedule. Do you usually have early morning breakfast meetings? Do you have to spend evenings preparing dinner? Try different times of the day, and keep track on your calendar of when and how far you walk. Then, after a few weeks, you can look back to see in which time slots your walking seems to fit best.

If you cannot mark off blocks of time in your day, there are plenty of unexpected ways to sneak walking into your schedule. In our "Cars are king" society, most cities and towns are not set up to facilitate walking, but that should not stop you from trying to figure out how you can make more use of your feet.

Consider, first of all, the possibility of walking to work. On the average, more than 5.6 percent of the working population in the United States uses this method of commuting, which has spawned a whole new fashion look in the cities—sneakers paired with business suits. You can see both men and women sporting the new style, but women seem most pleased by the acceptability of sneakers, since it liberates them from those torturing high heels—at least outside the office—and probably saves them hundreds of dollars in podiatry bills.

If you do not live close enough to walk to work, you can get off your bus or leave your car pool ten blocks early and walk the rest of the way. If you have to drive, park your car a half mile or a mile from the office and walk. Or if you commute by train, walk from the station to your place of employment instead of using the bus or a taxi.

Another way to carve out walking time is during your lunch break, which is just what Consuelo Perez, sixty-one, of Chicago does. "I use up twenty-three minutes of my lunch break doing my two miles. I come back, have my yogurt at my desk, and my adrenaline is really flowing. I get so much work done in the afternoon," she says.

You can also squeeze in some extra exercise by taking the stairs instead of the elevator whenever possible. If you are going up to the fifth floor of your favorite department store via escalator, don't just stand there, move—at least when you are not blocked by other shoppers who would rather stop than step. You can sometimes weave your way in between these standers, which may give them the hint that there is no law that says just because a stairway moves, you can't.

You could also leave your car at home and take out your walking shoes anytime you have to go to the corner store. "I don't take the car into town anymore," says Ed Smith, seventy-four, an avid walker who lives a few miles from the center of Morristown, New Jersey. "I walk up and back; it's terrific." If you don't live close enough to walk to town, drive up, park your car about a half mile or so away, and do all your errands on foot. You need never again do your errands by moving your car in front of every store you need to stop at.

Those personal cassette players with headphones are a real boon to walkers. They can make your walking time much more productive, and thus you will feel better about making room for walking in your schedule. Instead of sitting to watch a soap opera or television special, tape-record it; then listen to it later on a cassette player as you walk. If you are an avid reader, you can buy "talking books," entire books recorded on cassette tapes, and listen to them on your headset. Or if you have always wanted to learn a foreign language, you can buy self-instruction tapes and be speaking French—or whatever—in no time.

The key to fitting walking into your day is to *think ex-*

ercise! For a change, look at ways you can use calories instead of conserve them. Use a push lawn mower instead of a riding one. Rather than trying to carry three bags of groceries in from the car at once, make two trips. Instead of having friends over for coffee and cake, invite them over for a short walk and some juice and light snacks afterward. You can still visit with one another while you walk, and I'm willing to bet that the conversation will be livelier and spirits higher after you get a little blood flowing. When children come for a visit, don't automatically pull out the Monopoly game; pull them outside for a walk to show them the new puppy that lives down the street or for a game of hide-and-seek.

Where to Walk

Now that you have an idea of how to solve the "when to walk" problem, the next thing is to decide where to walk. If possible, choose a route close to your home that is away from vicious dogs and busy highways. It should not have too many hills—at least not while you are just starting out—and it helps to be surrounded by some pretty scenery. Pleasant distractions like flowers, birds, squirrels, and trees will make your walk seem much faster because such distractions get your mind off the work your body is doing. Studies have shown that people who exercise without distractions don't progress in their fitness programs as quickly as those who exercise in scenic surroundings.

"If you follow a regular route, you really begin to know certain trees and shrubs and notice how they change during the seasons. It's a real treat," says Martin Diaz, seventy-one, of Boston. If you do not live in an area that you feel is pretty or safe to walk through, drive to a park and do your walking there. However, be aware that you are more likely to stick to your walking route if it starts right at your front doorstep.

Many fitness experts and foot specialists (podiatrists) recommend that you walk on soft surfaces such as cinder tracks or grass because they are easier on your feet. However, some people prefer to walk on pavement because it gives them better traction and more stability. "When I walk on flagstone or asphalt, I just glide along,'' says Bob Bernstein. ''But when I walk on grass, I just can't get up the same speed.'' Try walking on different surfaces to see what feels best to you. If you do walk on grass, it is best not to go through the middle of a field or pasture, since you may fall into hidden holes or trip over unseen rises in the terrain. Stick to the grass along sidewalks and roads or in parks. If you'd rather walk on pavement, do so on a sidewalk or on a track, and make sure your shoes are especially well cushioned.

If you must walk on the street because you do not have sidewalks in your area, make sure that you walk along the side, facing oncoming traffic. You do not want cars sneaking up behind you. If you are walking with a friend, you should go single file along the edge of the road, and never, no matter how deserted you think the road is, walk in the middle of the street. Who knows what is going to come cruising around the next curve?

There may be times—when it is raining or cold, for instance—when you may want to walk indoors. You can go to an indoor track or a gym, but probably a better choice as far as scenery goes is a shopping mall. ''When it's very cold out or when there's high humidity or heat, I walk in a mall,'' says Sal Ricca, fifty-nine, who walked throughout his recovery from a heart attack. ''I like it because I can do my three miles in a controlled environment. It's always about seventy degrees inside.''

Malls are becoming popular walking places, and some mall operators are even encouraging people to exercise under their roofs. Since 1983, the Foothills Mall in Maryville, Tennessee, has opened every morning at seven o'clock, three hours earlier than the stores inside, so that morning walkers have a safe, weather-protected place to exercise. Two laps around the 600,000-square-foot mall equals approximately one mile, and the mall has painted distance markers every quarter of a mile. About forty-five people—most of them over age forty—walk the mall in the morning on a regular basis. Many people walk indoors in the winter so that they don't have to deal with the cold. In the summer, walkers head for the mall to escape the heat.

What to Wear

This is easy—you can wear whatever you are comfortable in. Of course, what you wear will depend on the weather (see chapter 12) and whether you are walking inside or out. Just make sure you have a good pair of shoes (see chapter 10) and that your clothes are loose-fitting. Avoid girdles and tight, elasticized arm openings. You may want to loosen your belt while you walk to help you breathe more deeply.

Some walkers like to go out in their street clothes so that they don't call attention to themselves. Others, however, find that wearing exercise togs, such as a warm-up suit or running shorts, makes them feel that they have *really* exercised.Some people like to wear exercise clothes so that they *look* as if they have worked out. Just remember that there is no substitute for actually doing it.

Ten Top Walk-to-Work Cities
(Based on percentage of
total work force 16 years and older)

Rank	City	Total Work Force	Walk to Work	% of Total
1	Boston, MA	250,050	41,472	16.6
2	San Diego, CA	419,332	51,626	12.3
3	Pittsburgh, PA	164,830	19,122	11.6
4	Washington, DC	295,131	33,813	11.5
5	New York, NY	2,824,989	320,308	11.3
6	San Francisco, CA	336,627	36,823	10.9
7	Philadelphia, PA	608,391	64,005	10.5
8	Newark, NJ	104,428	11,014	10.5
9	Buffalo, NY	126,358	19,122	10.0
10	Minneapolis, MN	183,689	16,446	9.0

Source of Information: U.S. Bureau of the Census, 1980 Census of Population, *General Social and Economic Characteristics* (Series PC80–1–C).

Walking for a Living

Pauline Semol, sixty-nine, of New York City, walks ten miles a day—and gets *paid* for it! Pauline is a messenger with Archer Messenger Service in Manhattan. For four hours a day, she walks all over the city delivering packages to offices in skyscrapers, then returning to the messenger service office to pick up new assignments. "It's hard to believe I'm getting a check to do my hobby," she says.

In 1984, Pauline began walking half a mile a day to fight a weight problem and gradually worked her way up to longer distances. At a walking race sponsored by Archer Messenger Service four months after she started her program, she walked one mile in thirteen minutes. After that race, she began thinking that it would be fun to be a messenger, and when she asked at Archer about a job, she was happy to learn that the company hired retirees. She started work the following Monday. "Before this, I was doing clerical work just to keep busy," she says. "This is a real challenge."

Pauline is one of about 120 older messengers, or 12 percent of the staff, at Archer. Retirees usually prefer working part-time—four to five hours a day—says Ed Davis, the hiring manager for Archer. They mostly carry envelopes and light packages. David reports that the retirees are some of Archer's best employees. "Most have retired from very good jobs; we find they're very trustworthy and reliable. They have good training, a good background," he reports. "And they're happy working here too. They're tired of sitting home or sitting in the park. This keeps them active and useful."

Check at messenger services in your city to find out if they hire retirees. Maybe you, too, could be getting paid and getting fit at the same time.

(3)

How Much, How Soon, How Often

You may know someone like him. He tells everyone he's taking up tennis. He talks endlessly about the racket he just bought, the number of lessons he takes each week, the progress on his backhand, the tennis camp he will attend. He hurls himself into the sport, playing every chance he gets with seemingly boundless energy and enthusiasm. Then after a while, you stop hearing about his serve and his volley. You don't miss the detailed description of every stroke, but you just wonder what happened.

What happened is something that commonly occurs when someone takes up a new activity. There is an initial flush of excitement; then it's as if he or she overdoses on it. The problem is doing too much too soon. This can happen with any new undertaking, including walking, especially after you get charged up reading about all of walking's benefits. The tendency might be to go out and try to make up for all the time you didn't exercise. So, instead of starting at a mile, you take off on a brisk three-mile walk the very first day. You may be able to keep this up for a short while, but eventually your body is going to scream for you to take it easy. Most bodies do not adapt to sudden increases in physical activity that quickly. If you've been sedentary for years, you especially need to build up slowly to such a pace. Many cardiologists and exercise physiologists suggest that you not expect drastic changes in your activity level for a minimum of three months. Your patience will pay off.

There is nothing wrong with enthusiasm, and I hope you will feel it for walking. However, be sure that in your exuberance you don't overlook what is best for your body. Start off your program safely. Determine how much you should be doing and when so that your walking shoes don't end up in the back of the closet like your friend's tennis racket, and your health doesn't end up suffering.

What Shape Are You In?

It is crucial to determine your physical condition before you start walking, which is why every walking program should begin with a trip to a doctor, particularly if you have ever had a heart problem or tightness in your chest or if you are overweight or have a chronic disease such as emphysema or diabetes.

Explain to your doctor that you want to get in shape through a walking program. He or she should conduct a complete physical examination that includes blood tests, particularly a cholesterol count; an update of your medical history; and readings of your resting heart rate and your blood pressure. It is most important that the doctor give you an exercise stress test or tell you where you can get one. For this, the physician may refer you to a cardiologist in private practice, a hospital cardiology department, or the physical education department of a major university.

An exercise stress test is a measure of your heart's performance while it is working hard during exercise. Blood pressure, heart rate, and respiration are measured, and the electrical impulses that control the beating of the heart are recorded on an electrocardiograph, which is hooked up to you while you exercise. Here are five good reasons to have a stress test, according to Dr. Kenneth H. Cooper, often called the father of aerobic exercise.

1. To help determine whether you have heart disease. The theory is that when your heart is under stress, it is more likely to show signs of disease or problems that otherwise might go undetected when you are going about your daily business, or when an electrocardiogram (ECG) is taken while you're resting. Dr. Cooper cites a recent report noting that persons who perform well on the exercise part of the test have a significantly better long-term chance of avoiding a heart attack or sudden death. A poor performance on the stress test doesn't conclusively point to heart disease; other risk factors must be considered and further testing done to determine how fit your heart is.

Although the effectiveness of the stress test at predicting heart disease has been debated in the medical world, Dr. Cooper believes that if a test is administered and interpreted properly, it can provide valuable information, and he reports that at his Aerobic Center in Dallas, the stress test is accurate 80 percent of the time.

2. To have a record for future reference. If you have a stress test every year, which many doctors strongly recommend for anyone over forty, your doctor will be able to compare your results annually. If your performance suddenly worsens, your doctor will be alerted that a problem exists or is developing in your cardiovascular system.

3. To help your doctor prescribe a safe and effective exercise program. Your performance will give your physician a more precise idea of what level of exercise you can withstand.

4. To provide motivation. By having a test every year, you can measure your improvement, which can give you the boost you need to keep up your good work.

5. To monitor recovery or identify additional problems after a heart attack.

Stress tests are given on either a treadmill or a stationary bicycle, but many experts prefer the treadmill. "The [bicycle] seat is uncomfortable for many older adults. . . . In addition, if the quadriceps fatigue quickly, the cardiovascular system will not be maximally stressed," says Dr. Everett L. Smith of the University of Wisconsin. "Since walking is a natural activity, people adapt easily to the treadmill."

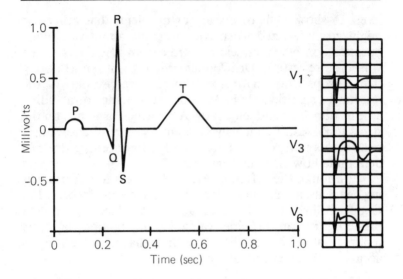

The ECG pattern on the left is for a normal heart; the electrocardiogram on the right shows typical ECG findings for the ST segment of myocardial infarction. The ST segment plunged instead of going up during the early stages of a treadmill stress test.

This is what the test entails: The person administering the test will attach several small electrodes at various points on your body. These electrodes are usually metal disks about the size of silver dollars attached to wires that will pick up your heartbeat and muscle activity. At least seven electrodes should be used; any less may not provide an accurate test. The electrical impulses of the heart are sent to the electrocardiograph, which records the impulses on a continuously moving roll of graph paper. A normal heartbeat will create a line with small waves in it and one large, sharp spike that rises upward on the graph.

You will generally start a stress test by walking on a level treadmill. In the most common test given, called the Bruce Protocol, the person administering the test will raise the incline of the treadmill and increase the speed every three minutes. With another method, the Balke Protocol, the incline is increased every minute, but the speed remains constant.

In a maximal stress test, you'll continue exercising at higher work loads until your electrocardiogram shows an irregularity or until you just can't go on anymore. Other symptoms that may cause the doctor to stop the test is a drop in blood pressure or the development of angina—pain in the chest or in the neck, throat, shoulder, or left arm. The number of heartbeats per minute when you reach your work capacity limit is called your maximum heart rate. The heart rate you should aim for when you exercise is 60 to 70 percent of that maximum; this is called your target heart rate. You should never exercise at your maximum heart rate except on this stress test. It would be dangerous to do so without medical supervision.

In a submaximal stress test, the doctor will have estimated your maximum and target heart rates before you start based on your age and resting heart rate. Then the doctor will have you exercise until your heart rate reaches the target level. Although some doctors consider this method safer because it is not putting such a strain on your heart, others believe that a submaximal stress test is less reliable. "If you stop at less than 85 percent of your maximum heart rate, that decreases the sensitivity and accuracy of the test," says Dr. Cooper. He adds that after giving more than 70,000 tests at his clinic over the past twenty years, he has not had a death associated with maximal stress testing.

There is a simple formula to determine your target heart rate. This formula should only be used as a general guideline for people over fifty. It should not be substituted for an exercise stress test, since it does not take into consideration health problems or medication that may affect your heart rate. The calculated range may be far off from your actual safe exercise level. Subtract your age from 220 to get your maximum heart rate, and then take 60 to 75 percent of that number to figure your target heart rate. (Although you may have heard that you should take 70 to 85 percent of your maximum heart rate to get your target range, many doctors recommend that people over fifty exercise at a slightly lower intensity.) Here, for example, is the calculation for a sixty-year-old.

$$220 - 60 = 160 \quad \text{(your approximate maximum heart rate)}$$

$$160 \times .60 = 96$$

$$160 \times .75 = 120$$

$$96 \text{ to } 120 = \text{(your approximate target heart rate range)}$$

A stress test is not inexpensive, but when you consider the information it can give you—whether you are currently suffering from coronary heart disease, your risk of developing coronary artery disease in the future, and what kind of exercise program you should follow—it is an exceptionally good value. The cost of a stress test ranges from $100 to $225. Generally, tests taken at the physical education department of a major university are the least expensive, those administered by a cardiologist in private practice the most expensive. You may want to go to a hospital for a test because Medicare generally covers diagnostic tests given in a hospital but not necessarily those given in a doctor's office.

How Fast Should You Walk?

You should walk at the speed that puts your heart rate in your predetermined target zone. At this level, walking becomes aerobic exercise, which is defined by Dr. Cooper as "those activities that require oxygen for prolonged periods and place such demands on the body that it is required to improve its capacity to handle oxygen." As a result of aerobic exercise, beneficial changes occur in the lungs, the heart, and the vascular system. Cooper determined that to get aerobic benefit, you should not walk any slower than your target heart rate. To avoid straining your body, you should not walk much faster. This does not mean that your heart rate must be exactly on the target number; it can generally be in a range five beats above or below it.

As you get in better condition, your heart rate will drop below the target range, even though you are exercising as hard as before. This is a sign that your heart has adapted to the exercise, and it is time to increase your speed. But even when you pick up the pace, your heart rate will probably not rise above your target range because your heart will have become more efficient and will be able to do more work in the same number of beats. What this means is that if you start off walking two miles per hour at your target heart rate of 125, you may eventually get to the point where you can walk three miles an hour with your heart still beating 125 times per minute.

It is important that you monitor your heart rate while you walk to make sure that you are walking at a safe speed. You can determine your heart rate by finding your pulse at the underside of your wrist. You should feel the throbbing of the blood moving through your body. While looking at the second hand or the digital display of your watch, count the number of beats over ten seconds. Now multiply that number by six, and you get your heart rate per minute. For example, if you count out 18 beats, your heart rate per minute is 108. Make sure you have a good watch; you may want to get a heart rate monitor (see chapter 11).

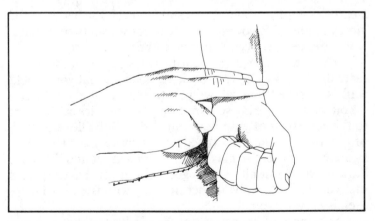

To take your pulse accurately, press the index finger and the third finger of one hand firmly against the wrist just below the thumb of the other hand.

One cautionary note: You may see an exerciser taking his or her pulse at the carotid artery on the side of the neck. Although you can feel your pulse at this point, some fitness experts discourage people from using it. "The two carotid arteries on either side of the neck are the only blood supply to the brain. If a person blocks one off while trying to get a pulse, he or she may pass out," says Kate Booth, director of the Morristown Memorial Hospital Cardiac Rehabilitation Center in Morristown, New Jersey. "Plus, if in their effort to find their pulse, they massage their neck, their heart rate will usually drop. Doctors massage the neck when they want to lower someone's heart rate." Getting a lower reading could cause you to exercise above your target heart rate without realizing it, which is particularly dangerous for older people.

Take your heart rate before you start off on your walk; this is your resting heart rate. Take your heart rate again five minutes into your walk. (Walk in place while you do this, so that you don't trip while your eyes are fixed on your watch.) If your pulse is lower than your target heart rate, pick up your step a bit. If it is higher than your target rate, slow down. Take your heart rate again at the end of your walk and again about ten minutes after you have done your cool-down exercises. (See pages 44–48.) The more quickly your heart rate returns to your preexercise level, the better condition you are in. If your heart rate is not within two counts of your preexercise level, continue to rest.

There are other, less scientific ways of determining how fast you should walk. One basic guideline is that you should walk at a speed that allows you to talk during your walk. "You may be working so hard that your muscles can't adapt to the new stress of your workout," says Bob Glover, coach of a nationally ranked women's running team. "They may tighten; your exercise may become unpleasant and difficult. Slow down. After all, what's good about aerobic exercise is that you can do it while jabbering away with friends who are exercising with you."

Shortness of breath is another indicator that you are walking too fast. You should be able to breathe deeply and comfortably thoughout your workout. Also, a walk at a good, brisk pace should work up some perspiration. If you are not sweating at all, you probably are not walking as fast as you should be. But before you speed up, check your heart rate to make sure that it is indeed below the target level.

How Often Should You Walk?

You should walk at least four times per week, preferably on alternate days, and try not to skip more than two days in a row (you can start to lose muscle tone after three days without exercising). A recent study by Leonard Epstein and Rena Wing at the Western Psychiatric Institute and Clinic in Pittsburgh showed that exercise four or five times a week is significantly more effective than the same exercise performed three times a week. Some people find that walking every day is no problem because walking is a low-intensity exercise. It is probably best to start off at four times a week, then consider walking more often after you've walked at this frequency for at least three months.

How Far Should You Walk?

Remember the cigarette commercial where the rugged, road-weary traveler looked at the camera and said, "I'd walk a mile for a Camel." Note he didn't say, "I'd walk fifteen minutes for a Camel." When it comes to distances, you naturally think of feet, yards, and miles. In your walking program, it is better to think about minutes. It does not really matter how far you walk. It is how long you walk at your target heart rate that is important for improving fitness.

Walking for time makes choosing a route easier. If you start off by deciding to walk a certain distance, you have to go out in your car and mark off, say, one mile, or at least know a one-mile course. But if you are walking for time and you want to walk twenty minutes, you simply go out for ten minutes, than turn around and come home. If you would like, you can measure the route afterward to see what distance you have covered (or you could wear a pedometer, which measures the distance as you walk) and figure out your speed. Walking for time is also helpful when you go out on a route that gets you home before your twenty minutes, for instance, are up. You simply go around the block a few more times until you have used up the time. This is where a good watch is important. You might want to get one that has a stopwatch function; you can set it as you start out, and you will know exactly when you should finish your walk.

Based on the results of your stress test, your doctor should be able to give you a good idea of how much you should do to begin with. He or she may suggest starting out at ten minutes just to be safe if you have some health problems. If you are in relatively good shape, you can probably start at twenty minutes, as suggested in the walking program outlined on page 33. Your goal is to walk at least forty-five minutes four times a week; you should try to cover at least three miles in that time. The suggested walking program shows you how to work up to this pace safely. Although twenty minutes of aerobic exercise per session is usually considered enough to condition your body, you generally have to walk for a longer time because walking is a less strenuous exercise.

If You Do Too Much Too Soon

You will feel it if you overdo it—in your muscles mainly. Although your muscles may be mildly sore even if you are progressing at a safe pace, you will know you have done too much if they are painfully sore and you have one or more of the following complaints: headache, sore throat, unusual fatigue, problem falling asleep, irritability, or lowered resistance.

Sore muscles are your body's way of telling you that something's wrong. Soreness indicates that the muscle needs repair, and as you age, your muscles, joints, and tissues don't repair themselves as quickly as when you were younger. When you don't allow your body to recover, you get overtired—so overtired that your body actually has trouble settling down to sleep.

Don't sabotage the benefits of walking by doing too much too soon. Remember, it took years for your body to slide into the condition it is in now; don't expect to whip it back into shape in a few weeks. Take it easy, and building good health will be easy as well.

Suggested Walking Exercise Program
(50 Years of Age and Older)

Week	Distance (miles)	Time Goal (minutes)	Frequency / Week
1	1.0	20:00	4
2	1.5	30:00	4
3	2.0	40:00	4
4	2.0	38:00	4
5	2.0	36:00	4
6	2.0	34:00	4
7	2.5	42:00	4
8	2.5	40:00	4
9	2.5	38:00	4
10	3.0	47:00	4
11	3.0	46:00	4
12	3.0	45:00	4

(4)

How to Walk

But I learned how to walk when I was ten months old!'' may be the first thing to come to mind upon reading the title of this chapter. "Don't you just put one foot in front of the other?" Sure, you can follow that technique as long as you are only walking a few yards here, a quarter mile there. If you are going to undertake a serious distance walking program, however, you will want to take a serious look at what makes your body go.

Because walking seems to be a simple activity, you have probably never thought about what your body does during each step. Walking is actually a complex activity involving a number of factors including the use of hip and knee muscles, the quadriceps, the buttocks, the hamstrings, calf muscles, and a variety of other muscles, bones, and ligaments; it is a well-synchronized cycle that has the whole body moving together in harmony.

When you walk, your moving body is supported first by one leg, then by the other. As the body passes over the supporting leg, the other leg swings forward in preparation for its supporting role. One foot is always on the ground, and there is a period—after you put down the heel of your forward foot and before you pick up the toe of your rear foot—when both feet are on the ground, which gives you

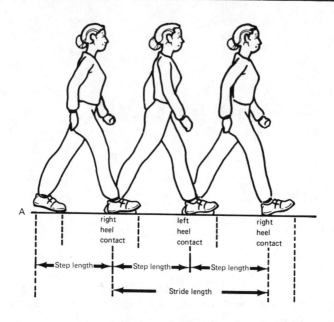

A

right
heel
contact

left
heel
contact

right
heel
contact

◄—Step length—► ◄—Step length—► ◄—Step length—►

◄————————— Stride length —————————►

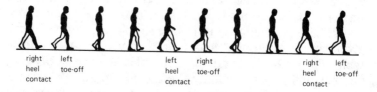

right   left
heel   toe-off
contact

left   right
heel   toe-off
contact

right   left
heel   toe-off
contact

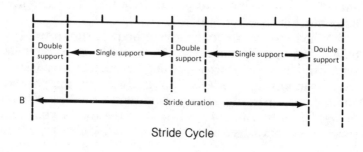

Double
support

◄—Single support—►

Double
support

◄—Single support—►

Double
support

B   ◄————————————— Stride duration —————————————►

Stride Cycle

extra stability. This is one reason walking is so much easier on your legs than running. In running, both feet are off the ground during a portion of each stride, and the force on each leg when the foot lands can be three to four times your body weight.

You may think that walking simply moves your body forward, but while you walk, your body actually moves up and down and side to side as well. As the body passes over the supporting leg, it rises until the foot is directly underneath and then descends again as the foot passes behind. The body also moves sideways over the supporting limb while the other leg is swinging forward. Women move their hips more than men do when they walk.

To get more out of your walking, there are several elements to concentrate on as you move along.

Proper Posture

One thing that may suffer as a person grows older is posture. The passage of time may make your shoulders and back rounder, which is the reason that keeping proper posture should be one of your main concerns while you walk. Even if you took your mother's admonition to "stand up straight" to heart (and spine) when you were younger and developed excellent posture, that posture may now be something less than perfect.

To develop proper posture, you could, of course, walk with a book on your head. Or you can follow these tips from Dr. Ash Hayes, executive director of the President's Council on Physical Fitness and Sports: In front of a mirror, stand straight with your feet pointing straight out in front of you, hip-width apart. A quick way to check whether your legs are properly aligned is to bend your knees slightly, keeping your upper body straight. Do your knees go straight out over your feet? If yes, you probably have strong lower legs. If your knees turn inward, you could have some lower-leg or knee problem. Such a condition can sometimes be accommodated with an orthopedic device.

Now, on with the posture positioning: Pull in your stomach muscles. Move the front of your pelvis up and the buttocks down and under so that the pelvis is vertical, not at an angle. You can check this posture in the mirror. "Seventy percent of lower back pain could be avoided if people exercised with the pelvis in the correct position," says Hayes. "But lots of people don't because their abdominal muscles are out of shape, and when you don't pull in those muscles, your pelvis isn't properly aligned." Pulling in your stomach muscles while you walk will help strengthen them.

Next, raise your chin and your chest, and pull your shoulders back; this position should not be tense, but relaxed. "That's the posture you should stand and walk in," maintains Hayes. In addition, remember that you shouldn't look down while you walk; it will help keep your posture in line if you look four to five yards in front of you.

Stride

A stride is the distance measured from the initial heel strike of one foot to the heel strike of the next foot and then to the next heel strike of the first foot—essentially two steps. The length of your stride is one determinant of your walking speed. Stride lengths range from about 89 percent of body height for slow walkers to 106 percent of body height for brisk walkers, but generally you can figure that stride length is about equal to your height.

The other determinant of walking speed is the number of steps taken per minute. Seventy to 130 steps per minute is the range of normal walking speed; a military march is 120 steps per minute.

Most people increase both their stride length and their step frequency to walk faster. If you want to pick up the pace, you don't have to start taking giant steps—this can put too much pressure on the pelvis—or try to go as fast as a windup toy. You will be able to make a noticeable difference in your walking speed by taking a few more steps per minute. This will increase your flexibility of motion, and the faster walking speed will become habit naturally. The increased flexibility will result in a longer stride length. This is because each person has a step rate and a stride length that his or her body feels most comfortable with and naturally goes to. It is generally a slower pace than you should walk at to gain maximum health benefits.

Foot Placement

When your foot comes in for a landing with a step, make sure your heel touches ground first, then the outside of your foot, and then onto the ball of your foot so that the foot is in position to push off again. Some people put the whole foot down at once, especially if they get tired, but this is more jarring to the body and makes the walking motion less fluid.

As your heel strikes, your foot and your ankle should make a ninety-degree angle. Be careful, though, that you don't overflex your foot. Pulling your foot too far back when you lower it to the ground can cause foot pain.

When you roll onto the ball of your foot, your toes should point out straight in front of you. Don't worry if your toes turn out a little bit, but a duckfooted walk can strain your knee joints and back. The opposite problem, pigeon-toed walking, can cause knee and ankle injuries. Duckfooted walkers may find that walking with their feet farther apart solves their problem. (Many overweight people walk duckfooted because of heavy thighs.)

Carriage

The way you carry your body is only partly a physiological matter; another major element is psychological. How you feel about yourself and the world in general is expressed through your walking form. Holding your head high and walking with a bouncy step says, "I feel great. I like myself." A draggy, slouchy style says, "I'd rather not be doing this." Someone who is uptight may walk with clenched toes and fists and tightened calves, creating a stiff form. Someone who is insecure or timid may walk with shoulders and head down.

Concentrate on your posture and try to think positive thoughts—how good this exercise is for you—and your carriage should improve.

Arm Swing

It is the feet that do the walking, but the arms do play an important part—they provide balance. When you step out with your left foot, your right arm will swing forward, and vice versa. Because your trunk rotates in the direction of the stepping foot, the swing of the opposite arm is necessary to counterbalance the movement and keep your trunk from rotating too far in one direction. Try walking with your arms straight by your side, and you will see how awkward and jerky walking would be if you didn't use your arms. Now try walking while you swing the same arm as your extended leg, and you will be able to feel how much the body rotates with each step and why you need the arms as balancers. Arm swinging also helps you keep the rhythm of your walking.

When you walk at a moderate pace, your arms will generally be straight when they swing. When walking fast, you might want to bend them at a ninety-degree angle and swing your fists up to shoulder height when you bring your arms forward. These shorter, quicker arm swings will enable your arms to go as fast as your legs. To promote upper body conditioning, exaggerate the arm swings and actually pump with your arms.

Breathing

Most people know how important breathing is, but again here is an activity, like walking, that is so instinctive you probably have never given the technique much thought. But you should, since most people breathe inefficiently when they exercise. The major problem is shallow breathing, when you partially fill your lungs with oxygen. When you breathe shallowly, you aren't taking in enough oxygen, and you can't get enough oxygen to your extremities. Nor are you getting rid of all the carbon dioxide that your muscles produce as a waste product.

You must learn how to breathe deeply, from down in your belly. It is important to get your lungs operating like a bellows in order to get the most oxygen into your body. Put your hand on your stomach and inhale deeply without lifting your chest so that your lower abdomen fills up with oxygen (your abdomen will push out), followed by your upper abdomen, then your chest. You can get air straight to your belly if you make an O with your mouth and suck in air strongly (you should hear a "whooshing" sound). When you exhale, your lower abdomen should empty out first (causing the abdomen to flatten out), then your upper abdomen, then your chest. Keep your mouth in an O when you blow the air out. Once you learn to breathe correctly, you will have more energy and endurance because more oxygen will be circulating throughout your body.

Another breathing problem that some people have is forgetting to breathe or holding their breath while they are exercising. Your breathing should be rhythmic and consistent. Because your muscles use oxygen constantly while you walk, they need a constant supply to keep your body moving efficiently.

To help you get some rhythm in your breathing, follow this synchronization: When you walk at a moderate pace, inhale every two steps and exhale every two steps; when you walk quickly, inhale every four steps and exhale every four steps. Or develop your own pattern, based on whatever feels comfortable to you. Establishing some kind of pattern will help you keep the pace of your walking consistent.

Balance

Good balance is something that you will especially want to concentrate on because your sense of balance may become less keen. This means that your risk of falling may become greater as you age. Developing proper walking techniques can help compensate for any loss in balance. Correct posture is of utmost importance because when you stand straight with your stomach muscles pulled in and your pelvis tucked under, your center of gravity is right below your navel, and this provides greater stability for the upright body. Also, be sure to concentrate on your arm swing as you walk and to place your feet firmly on the ground for better balance.

Perspiration

Walkers do perspire somewhat, but there's usually not the soaking sweat that you get with more vigorous exercises. Perspiration is a very healthy and essential function. It is part of the body's cooling system. Heat is produced by your moving muscles as they convert glucose to energy. To compensate, your sweat glands wet your skin so that as air passes over your body, the sweat evaporates and the body is cooled. Perspiration means that your body is functioning well and that you are getting a good workout. With regular exercise, this cooling system will become more efficient, keeping your body temperature more stable. One caution: As you get older, you don't work up a sweat as quickly, and your body takes longer to cool off. Also, when you are through exercising, it takes you longer to stop sweating than when you were younger. So don't overdo your outdoor exercising if it is hot out.

Warming Up and Cooling Down

It's an icy winter morning. You want to go shopping. You get into your car, which has been sitting outside overnight, and turn the key. Then what do you do? If you have any sense about engines, you will let the motor warm up before taking off. Running your car a few minutes before you pull out onto the road will get the oil circulating and the moving parts operating smoothly for a better, safer ride.

Now, why would anybody treat a car better than his or her own body? It happens quite often. People will frequently put on their exercise clothes and just jump right into walking, running, basketball—whatever—at full throttle. You know how a car coughs, sputters, and stalls if you don't warm it up properly; well, the same thing can happen to your body. It is possible that you don't engage in enough activity before you exercise to get the "juices" flowing, so your body may be as "cold" as a car that has sat outside overnight in freezing temperatures.

Warming up for five to ten minutes gets your heart pumping and increases your body temperature. "A cold muscle can be compared to a dry leaf found on the ground on a fall day. Any attempt to manipulate the leaf results in small tears and cracks," says Phillip J. Tyne, strength and flexibility coach for the San Diego Chargers, and Matt Mitchell in their book, *Total Stretching*. "A muscle that is fully pumped with a fresh supply of blood is more like the healthy green leaf picked from the tree in spring; the leaf can be bent and wadded in your hand, yet it springs back to its original shape without a single tear."

"Increasing coronary circulation is especially important in middle-aged and older adults, since myocardial ischemia [an insufficient blood supply to the heart] has been observed at the onset of strenuous exercise without preceding warm-up," says Dr. Paul Fardy, a cardiac rehabilitation specialist. Warming up is also important because it helps prevent muscle soreness and promotes greater flexibility of the joints.

The ideal procedure for warming up is to start with some gentle activity that will get your heart pumping faster, such as walking at a slow pace. You may want to do some stretching exercises also. You will get a better stretch and will reduce your chances of tearing muscles if you stretch after light exercise has caused more blood to be pumped to your muscles. You want to stretch only when your muscles are flexible and supple. On pages 44–48 are some warm-up and stretching exercises; many of them can be used after exercising for cooling down as well.

Cooling down is crucial because it safely eases your body to a lower level of activity. When you are walking, your blood vessels dilate, and if you stop completely, the blood in these enlarged vessels is pulled downward by gravity. It comes out of the brain, away from the heart and vital organs, and could cause a person to become light-headed. A heart attack victim could get angina because the reflex of the heart in this case is to pump faster to get the blood back up.

Don't stop suddenly when your walk is over. Walking at a slow pace can help the heart circulate the blood adequately as you cool down gradually and the vessels return to their normal size. Then you might do some stretching exercises. Cooling down properly—it takes about five or ten minutes—also helps prevent muscle cramps and will help you develop longer, more limber muscles instead of hard, tight ones.

Warm-Up and Cool-Down Exercises

To prepare your body for a good walk, you may want to do the following exercises. Exercises 1–2 are used to bring more blood, and in turn more oxygen, to your muscles and should be done first. The rest of the exercises are for stretching various muscles of your body. To get maximum benefit, do these exercises in succession without pausing. Exercises 3–12 are also excellent cool-down activities.

Unless otherwise noted, begin by standing with shoulders back and relaxed and your spine straight. Pull in your abdominal muscles (don't forget to breathe regularly even though your abdominal muscles are tight), bend your knees slightly, and tuck in your buttocks. Your pelvis should be held straight, not at an angle. If you cannot do as many repetitions as suggested, do what you can, and try to work up to the recommended number. None of these exercises should cause discomfort. If you experience pain, stop the exercise and consult your physician.

1. *Arm swings.* Bend forward slightly at the waist and look at the floor. Your feet should be shoulder-width apart. Swing your right arm straight back and your left arm forward. Then swing the right arm forward and the left arm back. Begin to bend your knees and straighten them so that your bouncing is coordinated with your arm swings. Repeat twenty times.

2. *Arm circle-steps.* Stand with your feet a few inches apart. Raise your arms at your sides to shoulder level. Make a fist with each hand, and move your fists in small circles. At the same time, step from side to side. Take ten side-to-side steps while your arms are moving in forward circles. Repeat ten times, using backward circles.

Now that your muscles are warmed, you can begin stretching. A word of caution, however: Always proceed slowly and gently; never bounce. The purpose of stretching is to elongate and relax the muscles and tendons. Hold most stretches for at least thirty seconds. If you bounce, your muscles contract with each bounce, causing them to tighten and shorten.

3. *Neck stretches.* Move your chin toward your chest and hold ten seconds. Then lift your chin and move your head backward, looking up at the ceiling. Hold ten seconds. Next, try to bring your right ear as close to your right shoulder as possible, but do not lift your shoulder. Then bring your left ear toward your left shoulder. Hold each position for ten seconds. Repeat five times.

4. *Shoulder shrugs.* Lift your shoulders, bringing them as close to your ears as possible. Hold five seconds; then relax. Repeat five times.

5. *Overhead stretches.* Stand with your feet shoulder-width apart. Put your hands together in front of you, and intertwine your fingers; then turn your palms down. Stretch your arms out and raise them over your head, keeping your hands clasped. Stretch your palms toward the ceiling as far as you can, raising up on your toes. Hold thirty seconds. Bring your heels back to the floor. Next, bend to the right side, stretching your arms to the right. You should feel the stretch down your left arm and the left side of your body. Then bend to the left, stretching your right side. Hold each side stretch thirty seconds. Bring your arms back over your head and then down in front of you. Repeat five times.

6. *Side stretches.* Stand up with your feet shoulder-width apart, with your hands at your sides. While facing forward, slowly slide your right hand down your leg toward your knee, bending to the right as far as possible. At the same time, slide your left hand up your body to mid-chest level. This will stretch the left side. Now slide your right hand up your body, and your left arm down, stretching the right side. Repeat five times.

7. *Torso twists.* Stand with your feet shoulder-width apart. Bring your hands up to your chest, holding your arms and elbows parallel to the floor. It is especially important on this exercise that your buttocks be tucked, your pelvis straight, and your stomach muscles pulled in. Twist slowly at the waist to one side, keeping your hips facing straight ahead. Look in the direction you are moving. When you have twisted as far as you can, turn to the center and twist in the other direction. Only your upper body should move; your lower body should not. Repeat ten times.

8. *Bend-over stretches.* Stand with your feet a few inches apart and your hands at your sides. Bring your chin toward your chest, bending your neck forward. Slowly, roll your shoulders forward, and lower your head toward the floor, letting your arms hang loose in front of you and keeping your legs straight. The purpose of this exercise is to stretch gently your spine and the muscles of your back. Always move slowly (taking about thirty seconds for the forward bend), and never go further than is comfortable. When you reach your maximum stretch, hold for thirty seconds. Then, again slowly, unroll upward. Keep your chin tucked as your return to an upright position. When your back is straight, raise your chin out of the tucked position.

If you would like, you can do this stretch while sitting in a chair. Sit straight up, then tuck your chin, and proceed as you would above, bending over as far as you can and trying to get your fingers close to the floor.

9. *Foot warm-ups.* You can do this exercise while standing (you may want to stand against a wall or hold on to a couch or chair for balance) or sitting in a chair. Hold one foot out in front of you a few inches above the floor. Rotate the foot five times clockwise, then five times counterclockwise. Repeat with the other foot. Next, point one foot forward as you hold it out in front of you. Then bring your toes toward the body and push out with the heel, stretching the calf muscle. Hold the flex for five seconds. Point and flex five times with each foot.

10. *Achilles tendon stretches.* Stand about two or three feet from a wall, facing it. Place your hands on the wall at about shoulder height. Slide your right foot back about twelve to fourteen inches, keeping the toes pointed straight ahead. Next, bend your left knee (the forward leg) slightly, and lean toward the wall. Be sure to keep the heel of your right foot (the rear foot) on the floor and the leg straight. Keep your hips facing straight ahead. You will feel the stretch along your calf muscle and Achilles tendon. Hold for thirty seconds to two minutes. Repeat with the left leg back. (If you cannot keep your heel down on this stretch, slide your back foot forward slightly.)

11. *Hamstring stretches.* Stand three to four feet from a wall, facing it with your feet pointed forward. Slide your right foot back about ten inches. Bend forward at the waist, keeping your back and both legs straight. You should feel the stretch at the backs of your thighs. Bend over as far as possible, but not lower than waist level. Be sure to keep your back straight the whole time and both heels on the floor. If you need help keeping your balance, put your hands on the wall in front of you, but do not push against the wall. If this stretch is too difficult, move your feet farther apart. Hold the stretch for a minimum of thirty seconds. Repeat with your left leg back.

12. *Calf stretches.* Facing a wall, stand with your feet pointed straight ahead. Place your hands on the wall at shoulder height. Slide your right foot back two to three inches. Bend both knees, but bend your right knee a little more, lowering it toward the floor. Hold for thirty seconds, keeping both heels on the ground. You should feel the stretch in the calf muscle and quadricep (the muscle running on top of your thigh) of the front leg. Repeat with your left leg held back.

Women and Walking

Walking is an especially good exercise for women. Many women, especially older women, feel that exercise is somehow unfeminine. Of course, there is nothing unfeminine about caring for your health and improving your body, but for those women who do not feel comfortable getting out on the track or the tennis court and working up a heavy sweat, walking can be the answer. There is much for women to like about walking: they don't have to be athletes to participate, no special clothing is needed, and it is a relatively low-sweat activity.

There are some differences, though, in the way women and men walk—something you probably already suspected from observing people on the street. Women's shorter legs mean shorter strides, but women usually take more steps per minute than men do. The average step rate for women is 118 steps per minute and for men 112 steps per minute. Women swing their arms less and their hips more than men. Men, though, generally move the head and shoulders more as they walk. Some experts think that women swing their hips more because of their wider pelvises, while others think it is more a cultural adaptation—girls learn to swing their hips after seeing other women do the same. Also, putting one foot in front of the other as a woman walks in high-heeled shoes contributes to the swing.

High-heeled shoes change the way a woman walks. Women wearing such shoes take shorter steps and increase their step rate, and Dr. David Winter, a professor of kinesiology at the University of Waterloo in Canada, reports that it requires 60 to 70 percent more energy to walk in shoes with high heels than in flat shoes. Also, high heels are a real danger to walkers. They can cause lower-back problems and increase the chances of twisting an ankle. Extended wear can actually shorten a woman's Achilles tendon; ironically, this can make wearing flat shoes uncomfortable. You can avoid this problem by not wearing high heels exclusively and by avoiding them completely when walking for exercise. There is no doubt that flat shoes are what you should wear when you walk.

(5)

Walking for Your Heart

She was about sixty-five, short, slender but sturdy, and had a headful of loose, wispy curls. Every morning while I was visiting a friend a few summers ago, she would come walking—no chugging—past the house at 10:00 A.M., just as Phil Donahue was saying on TV, "Until next time." I used to watch her storm past—arms churning, chest up, eyes fixed about six feet in front of her—and wonder what gave her that determination, that dedication. I found out the last day of my stay as I was getting ready to leave for the airport. While I was loading my suitcase in the car, I noticed her coming down the street in full stride. Just then a boy rode up beside her on his bike and asked her right out, "Hey, lady. Why are you walking so fast?" She smiled and between her regulated breathing replied, "Because I like my heart. [Inhale.] I want to keep it working." She pulled up her shoulders and disappeared around the turn of the road.

Good for her, I remember thinking with a smile. Good for her, for liking her heart and *showing* it. Even though I don't know anyone who would admit to not liking his or her heart, many people sure *act* as if they don't. They eat foods dripping with oil and fat, or they smoke, or they sit . . . and sit . . . and sit. These factors along with other risks,

51

such as a genetic predisposition to coronary problems and advancing age, are what make heart disease the number one killer in America. More than half a million deaths a year in the United States are attributed to heart disease—more than all cancers combined. In addition, 5.4 million Americans have symptoms of heart disease (and many don't know it). It costs in excess of $60 billion a year in medical bills, lost wages, and productivity.

Since heart attacks were first diagnosed in 1912, doctors have been diligently searching for ways to prevent them, and all the while one of the most effective tools has been right under all our noses, literally—our bodies, our *moving* bodies. Scientific reports reveal that a sedentary lifestyle is one of several factors that will increase the chances of coronary problems and, conversely, that exercise will help reduce the risks. These include two studies by noted medical researcher Dr. Ralph Paffenbarger of the Harvard University School of Public Health. One study, published in the *New England Journal of Medicine,* showed that longshoremen in California who were the most physically active on the job were less likely to suffer from heart disease than were their sedentary co-workers. Similarly, after studying 16,000 Harvard alumni and carefully noting, among other activities, their amount of daily walking, Paffenbarger reported in an article in the *Journal of the American Medical Association* that those who exercised regularly throughout their lives were less likely to develop heart disease than either those who never exercised or those who were active in college but not afterward. "If everyone had been physically active, there would have been a 23 percent lower incidence of coronary disease," concludes Paffenbarger. "People who are physically active live longer."

Fortunately, as the research pours out of universities and hospitals, people are pouring out onto the sidewalks, tracks, and courts and exercising to their hearts' delight—people who are at high risk of developing some form of heart disease, such as those with high blood pressure and elevated cholesterol levels; people who aren't at risk and want to stay that way; people who are recovering from heart attacks, like Sal Ricca.

Until February 13, 1984, Sal Ricca, a fifty-nine-year-old chemist from Summit, New Jersey, thought his heart was in fine shape. He had no reason to think otherwise—he didn't have high blood pressure, he wasn't overweight, and doctors told him he had the heart of a man fifteen years younger. Then on February 13, Sal had a heart attack. The cause? Atherosclerosis, the slow, silent buildup of plaque in the arteries that affects millions of Americans. Sal was one of the fortunate ones. He's here to talk about his heart problem and to be doing something to try to ensure that it never happens again—walking three miles, four to five days a week. "I'm still mad as hell that I had a heart attack," he says. "I've always been an active person, but I've never before been involved in a formal exercise program. There's a big difference. The walking I do now enriches me in so many ways. Besides making me healthier, it has given me a peacefulness; it has made me feel younger, and I definitely feel it's going to increase my life span. Heart surgery is not something I'm going to have to have. I'm convinced of that."

Cardiologists, too, are convinced of the value of walking and often prescribe the exercise for people who are recovering from heart attacks, for pacemaker patients, and for those who have symptoms of heart disease.

Walking is generally safer than other exercises for people with heart problems, especially for those persons who have been sedentary for years. Walking is not as taxing as other forms of exercise, and individuals can build up their endurance at a pace that their hearts can keep up with. Although some people move on to more strenuous forms of exercise, walking is often the recommended starting point. A study by Dr. K. Magnus and associates done in Wassenaar, the Netherlands, found that higher intensity exercise is not necessary or sometimes advisable for "tenderhearted" people. When heart attack victims who engaged in mild to moderate exercise such as walking added more vigorous exercise to their regular routines, it gave them little or no extra protection from acute coronary problems, the study determined. "Vigorous exertion may induce or exacerbate life-threatening arrhythmias in the middle-aged," the study states. "In view of this risk, vigorous exercise requires adequate screening and regular supervision. Those who find and take the opportunity to walk, cycle, or work in the garden, all the year round, are probably far better off."

How the Heart Works

The first step to improving your heart through walking is understanding the basics of how "the ole ticker" works. Sure, you probably learned this in your high-school biology class, but chances are it didn't matter to you then. Now that you are starting an exercise program, it does matter—even more so if you are at risk for heart disease or have had a heart attack. Knowing what happens in your body each time you hear that "ba-bump" will make you more attuned to your physical condition and the changes that exercise will bring.

The heart is a busy organ. During every minute of every hour of every year, as long as you live, your heart is continuously circulating blood to your muscles and organs. It beats an average of 100,000 times each day, pumping a total of 4,200 gallons of blood through 60,000 miles of blood vessels. In a lifetime, it will beat about 2.5 billion times and pump well over 100 million gallons of blood. It's exhausting just to think about it—and easy to see why you should be good to your heart! The pumping rate varies with the person and the activity level. When you're resting, it generally pumps about five liters of blood per minute, during exercise up to twenty-five liters per minute.

The heart, which is about the size of your fist and weighs less than a pound, sits in the center of the chest (not the left side, contrary to popular belief) and is divided into four hollow pumping chambers surrounded by powerful muscle tissue called the myocardium. The two upper chambers are called the left atrium and the right atrium; the two lower chambers are the left and right ventricles, which are larger and have thicker walls than the atria.

Blood flows through the heart along the route shown in the illustration. Blood depleted of oxygen from its trip

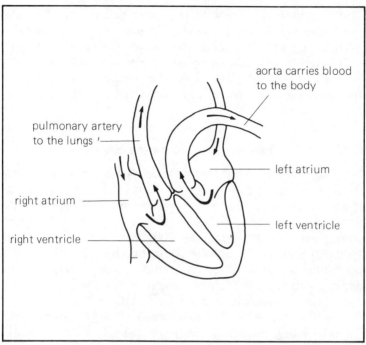

aorta carries blood
to the body

pulmonary artery
to the lungs

right atrium

right ventricle

left atrium

left ventricle

Blood moves from the right atrium of the heart to the right ventricle
and then to the lungs. From the lungs, it moves through the left side
of the heart and then to the body via the aorta.

through the body enters the right atrium, which contracts
and forces blood into the right ventricle. Now it's the right
ventricle's turn to contract, sending blood through the
pulmonary artery to the lungs. Here blood cells get refueled
with oxygen and then return to the heart through the left
atrium, which contracts and passes the blood to the left ventricle. When the left ventricle is filled with blood, it contracts strongly, causing blood to surge into the aorta, the
major artery supplying blood to the body. (All this goes on
in one beat. The softer "ba" is the sound of the atria contracting simultaneously; the louder "bump" is the sound of
the two ventricles contracting.)

The aorta then branches off into arteries that supply
blood to the brain, abdomen, arms, and legs. (There are

also two main coronary arteries that deliver blood to the heart muscle itself. It needs oxygen too!) The arteries branch out into tiny capillaries, which deliver the oxygen-rich blood to the cells and collect carbon dioxide, the waste product of the cells. The blood then makes its way back to the heart via the veins for more oxygen. And the whole circuit starts over again.

Effects of Aging on the Heart

It's a fact of life that as you get older, your heart isn't going to run as efficiently as it once did. One change that occurs in the heart as it gets older is a slowdown in the maximum rate at which it can beat. When you were eighteen, your heart could beat fast enough—say 200 beats a minute as you sprinted 500 yards uphill—to refuel muscles that were operating at full capacity, rapidly using oxygen and depleting their store of muscle sugar. Today, your heart just can't beat that rapidly, which is one of the reasons you can't go uphill as fast as you did as a teenager. The rough formula for calculating maximum heart rate for a healthy person is 220 minus your age. This means the maximum heart rate of someone fifty years old is 170; for a seventy-five-year-old, it's 145. Generally, maximum heart rate declines by approximately six to eight beats per decade. When you exercise, you shouldn't push yourself beyond 60 to 75 percent of your maximum to keep yourself within a safe activity level.

Work capacity also decreases with age. The flight of stairs you could climb with no problem when you were twenty-five may leave you feeling much more tired now that you're considerably past that age. Because your heart isn't working as efficiently or circulating blood as quickly, your heart rate may have to jump to 110 to enable muscles to get you up the stairs when before you could do it at a heart rate of 80. Also, your heart is known to get smaller with age, and the amount of blood pumped with each beat (stroke volume) is reduced.

Along with these changes, the efficiency of oxygen exchange in the lungs and the skeletal muscles decreases. Less of the oxygen you breathe in is actually absorbed by the blood because the heart is pumping less blood through the lungs. This means that less oxygen is getting to the muscles, which limits the intensity and duration of your activity. Dr. Steven Port and associates at Duke University Medical Center postulated that one of the possible causes of these cardiovascular changes is an age-related decline in the contractibility of the heart.

But there is encouraging news as well. A Duke University report by Dr. James A. Blumenthal and Dr. R. Sanders Williams states that "many of these [cardiovascular] changes are produced, even in young people, by prolonged physical inactivity. . . . A corollary of this hypothesis is the concept that increasing levels of physical activity in middle and later life significantly improve cardiovascular performance and prevent, or modify, the age-associated deterioration that has been observed in the elderly."

Effects of Exercise on the Heart

The major cardiovascular benefits of regular aerobic exercise are improved heart and lung efficiency and an increase in the body's work capacity. When you exercise, you stress the muscles of your skeleton and heart. With continued gradual increases in exercise, the body begins to adapt to the stress. This is called the "training effect," and it normally occurs after about six to eight weeks of regular aerobic exercise—sometimes after a little longer time for walkers. As a result of the training effect, the heart is able to supply the muscles with the oxygen and fuel they need with less effort.

Studies have found that when you exercise, your heart grows larger and becomes stronger, as does any muscle that is regularly exercised. This means that, with each beat, the heart is able to push more blood through your body, so it doesn't have to beat as many times to provide the muscles with the same amount of oxygen. In turn, this allows you to sustain your level of activity for a longer period of time or to increase your exercise intensity, or work capacity.

In addition, your resting heart rate should drop if you exercise regularly—so that when you take a breather on the living-room couch, your heart will be able to relax more too.

Again, this is because your heart can move the same amount of blood around with fewer beats. "Someone who is sedentary would tend to have a lower stroke volume," says Dr. Elliot Stein, a New Jersey cardiologist and exercise physiologist. "Someone who is physically active would have a larger stroke volume and would tend to compensate to a certain extent for the decrease in heart rate that comes with age."

For example, say you go out and walk briskly right now for a mile, and your heart rate goes up to 125. After several weeks of walking four times a week, you should be able to walk that same distance at the same speed with a lower heart rate (and feel less fatigued) because your heart won't have to beat as fast to maintain that pace. And the fact that walking works the muscles below the waist is especially important to your circulation; when these muscles contract and release in the walking motion, they force blood back up from the lower body, where it tends to pool.

According to Dr. Blumenthal and Dr. Williams of Duke University, exercise will increase your lung capacity, and your red blood cells will become more numerous. Thus, your body becomes more efficient at extracting and using oxygen from the bloodstream. On this note, a 1984 article by Robert A. Bruce of the University of Washington School of Medicine in *Medicine and Science in Sports and Exercise* stated that the decline in maximal oxygen uptake due to aging occurred twice as fast in sedentary men as in physically active ones. Bruce maintains that the health benefits of exercise on the heart can outweigh the common effects of aging. "Therefore," he says, "individuals may elect a life-style that is likely to diminish the rate of aging."

Bruce means an exercising lifestyle, and, guaranteed, it will be the most important "election" of your life. In addition, it could be the ticket to helping you head off two of the most serious—and most sneaky—health threats in the country: high blood pressure and atherosclerosis, both of which can cause fatal or debilitating strokes and heart attacks but often don't make their presence known until it is too late.

High Blood Pressure

You can feel hale and perfectly hearty and still have high blood pressure. The American Heart Association estimates that more than 34 million Americans—more than 10 percent of the adult population—have high blood pressure. And only half of these people are aware of it. High blood pressure, or hypertension, is a chronic elevation of the pressure in the cardiovascular system, which means that the heart is pumping harder than it should have to in order to get the blood through the body. When you have your blood pressure taken, a measuring gauge or digital readout records the pressure indicated by the level of mercury in a glass tube. The normal blood pressure reading when the heart beats, the systolic pressure, is generally between 100 and 140 mm Hg (millimeters of mercury) and is the first number given in a reading—for example, **139**/84. The normal reading when the heart rests, the diastolic pressure, is between 70 and 90 mm Hg, and is the second number given in a reading—for example, 139/**84**. As a person gets older, blood pressure tends to rise. The reason? With age, the arteries become harder, less elastic, and less able to withstand the pumping pressure. Thus, the force of each spurt of blood becomes more pronounced.

One of the more frightening aspects of high blood pressure is that no one really knows the causes of it. Doctors believe that heredity, stress, cigarette smoking, high salt intake, obesity, and lack of exercise each play a part, and they recommend that you correct as many of these factors as you can.

New research has found that making the change from a sedentary person to an exerciser is especially helpful in reducing blood pressure. After following 6,000 men and women over four years, Steven Blair and co-workers at the Institute for Aerobics Research in Dallas reported that those who were in poor physical condition increased their risk of developing hypertension by 50 to 60 percent compared to those in good condition.

In another study, Dr. Robert Cade and his research team at the University of Florida found that 101 out of 105 hypertensive patients had significant declines in blood pressure after following a regular exercise program—some by as much as 19 mm Hg—and more than half of the participants who were on antihypertensive medication before they started exercising were able to stop taking the drugs.

This should be of real interest to anyone who experiences unpleasant side effects from antihypertensive medication (headaches, lethargy, impotence, and dry mouth) and to anyone who is concerned about the toll drugs take on his or her budget. This investigation found that the patients who were able to get off medication saved an average of $3.36 per day on drug costs (or $1,226 per year). With exercise therapy, their cost fell to the price of one pair of good walking shoes a year. "This finding that exercise lowers blood pressure significantly in a group of sedentary hypertensive patients suggests that 'essential' hypertension [the most common type] is a result primarily of life-style and can be prevented or treated effectively by reasonable physical activity," the study concludes.

What makes exercise so effective in reducing high blood pressure? First, a lower heart rate means that your blood vessels take less of a pounding. In addition, exercise releases endorphins, brain chemicals that give you the euphoric exercise "high." Some scientists think these endorphins are closely related to substances that trigger the dilation of blood vessels, and more research is being conducted to determine whether endorphins have the same effect. It is possible, as medical experts often suggest, that the effect of exercise on high blood pressure could come from its influence on other high-risk factors, such as weight and stress reduction, rather than from the physical activity itself. But if in the process of easing anxiety, peeling off pounds, quitting smoking, or limiting alcohol consumption (once people start walking, they generally don't want to clog their lungs with smoke or make their muscles sluggish with alcohol), walking helps you bring down your blood pressure as well, it makes all the more sense to make it an integral part of your antihypertension action plan.

Coronary Artery Disease

Now, what about coronary artery disease, or atherosclerosis? The length of the name suits the enormity of the problem. Millions of Americans have atherosclerosis. Some physicians consider it the epidemic of the twentieth century—the plague of our overweight, overmechanized, underexercised society.

Atherosclerosis is a buildup of fatty deposit in the arteries. When it occurs in the coronary arteries, it can block the flow of oxygen-rich blood to the heart. It usually makes its presence known in one of two ways: angina pectoris, a tightness in the chest that occurs when a coronary artery is partially clogged, or a heart attack, which sometimes results in sudden death. Unfortunately, it is difficult to detect coronary artery disease before it gets to the point of being serious. For this reason, many doctors are telling their patients to take necessary precautions now—such as exercis-

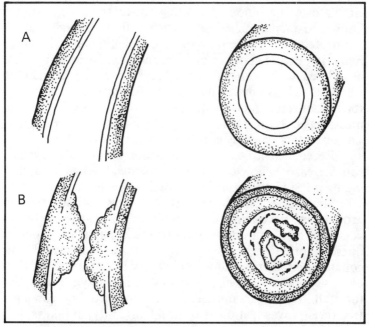

Coronary artery disease changes normal blood vessels. A normal coronary artery (A) may become blocked by the buildup of fatty deposits in a blood vessel (B). If this happens, the flow of blood to the heart is impeded.

ing, giving up smoking, losing weight, and lowering blood cholesterol levels.

Exercise is important because it can reduce the incidence of angina attacks, and, even more significant, it has been shown that a physically fit person is more likely to survive a heart attack than a sedentary victim—three times as likely, according to a study cited in *Boston University Medical Center's Heart Risk Book*. Then there's the exercise-cholesterol connection. Cholesterol, which is a dirty word in medical circles these days, is the main culprit of coronary heart disease and a substance that eggs, butter, bacon, and steak are rich in. Two types of cholesterol to be concerned with are low-density lipoproteins (LDLs) and high-density lipoproteins (HDLs). Low-density lipoproteins circulate in the blood, delivering fat to the cells, and are known to increase the risk of heart disease. High-density lipoproteins act as the scavengers of the circulatory system, removing excess cholesterol from the bloodstream, and are associated with *reduced* heart disease risk. To help lower levels of LDLs, many nutritionists suggest that you use fewer saturated fats—which are found in foods such as meat, eggs, butter, bacon and steak—and use more unsaturated fats, such as corn oil and safflower oil.

Recent scientific evidence indicates that regular exercise can decrease the low-density lipoproteins, the bad ones, and *increase* the high-density lipoproteins, the good ones.

Some scientists believe that exercise stimulates the growth or development of additional, collateral blood vessels, which can compensate to some extent for blocked ones. Another theory suggests that instead of stimulating collateral circulation, physical activity may enlarge existing coronary blood vessels, allowing more oxygen to pass through to the heart muscle despite any partial narrowings. In a recent investigation at Boston University, monkeys that were fed diets high in cholesterol and were exercised showed much less narrowing of the arteries than monkeys on a high-cholesterol diet that were sedentary. The exercising monkeys actually developed larger arteries.

Humans, too, have been able to reduce their cholesterol levels through exercise. In a cover story on cholesterol

Killer Cholesterol

Here are the levels of cholesterol (measured as milligrams per deciliter of blood) that the National Institutes of Health consider unsafe.

For People 40 and Over
  Moderate Risk: Greater than 240
  High Risk: Greater than 260

Average U.S. Daily Intake of Cholesterol in Milligrams
  Men: 500
  Women: 350

American Heart Association's Recommended Limit
  Men: 300
  Women: 225

that helped change the way many Americans feel about bacon and eggs, *Time* magazine profiled Fred Shragai, a fifty-nine-year-old real estate executive who, after suffering a heart attack and undergoing a coronary artery bypass operation, reduced his cholesterol level from 300 milligrams (per deciliter of blood) to a much safer 195 by giving up cholesterol-rich foods and walking eight miles every day. Dr. Charles Glueck, director of the University of Cincinnati Lipid Research Center, maintains that for every reduction of 1 percent in total cholesterol level, there is a reduction of 2 percent in risk of heart disease.

Cardiac Rehabilitation

Even for those who have serious heart problems, it's not too late to profit from walking regularly. Consider Fred Shragai and Sal Ricca, for instance. Here are two men whose heart attacks brought each close to death. But instead of adopting a "Well, it looks as if I'm doomed" attitude and giving up, which too many people do, they took their health in their own hands—and *feet*—and got in better shape than they had ever been in before.

Cardiac rehabilitation centers all across the country, which are increasingly prescribing exercise as part of the treatment, are filled with Fred Shragais and Sal Riccas, who want to avoid another heart attack or another bypass operation. They come out of desperation, they stay out of determination, and they improve out of dedication to a healthier lifestyle that often includes regular walking—the exercise of choice for many of these people because it's one of the only activities they *can* do following a heart attack or surgery.

The first rule of cardiac rehabilitation for anyone with a heart problem is, *Never* begin a walking program without a doctor's approval. Doctors often place heart patients in a hospital or community cardiac rehabilitation program, where they will have medical supervision while they do their walking. Another advantage of beginning in a rehabilitation center as opposed to setting out alone is the camaraderie that is present in a place where all participants are after the same goal—a healthier heart. The medical staff is there to boost heart patients' motivation and to teach them good nutrition, how to reduce other risk factors for heart disease, and proper ways to exercise.

For example, the Morristown (New Jersey) Memorial Hospital Cardiac Rehabilitation Center uses walking, among other exercises, and has about seventy-five patients in the program at any one time. Kate Booth, the director of the center, says that the majority of these are heart attack victims between fifty-five and sixty-five who have been inactive since they were thirty or so and eat too many of the wrong foods.

In the Morristown program, the effort to correct the damage done by years of this kind of living starts in the cardiac care unit with general health education, called Phase One. Phase Two includes limited exercise while in the hospital. About six to eight weeks after a heart attack, a patient can begin Phase Three as an outpatient and is given a submaximal stress test—an examination of heart function and heart rate under moderate exercise stress, as explained in chapter 3—to determine his or her target heart rate. Then it's on to low-level exercise for four to six weeks.

In Phase Four, the patient is given a *maximal* stress test (see chapter 3). "There is normally a great jump in the target heart rate between Phase Three and Phase Four," says Kate Booth. "That second stress test really gets them motivated. They get excited because by then they know what's good [in terms of their performance] and they can see how far they've come by exercising." Twelve weeks of training follows. Participants come into the center at least four times a week, warm up for five minutes, exercise at their target heart rate for at least twenty minutes (there's a track nearby for walkers and joggers), and then cool down for five minutes. If they have no problems, they can move on to the maintenance program, Phase Five, in which they have a choice of continuing their workouts at the center, going to a YMCA or health club, or exercising at home (the latter two choices require quarterly checkups at the center). The majority of patients reach this point six months after a heart attack, though some people will stay in the rehabilitation program for up to a year, depending on the severity of the heart problem each has.

Most doctors insist that heart patients start an exercise program in a rehabilitation center, but if there isn't a center nearby or if the patient can't afford to attend a program, some experts think it's all right to begin an unsupervised program at home *as long as* the exercise is walking and is done under a doctor's direction. Heart patients who do start an unsupervised walking program are advised to walk with others who know how to give cardiopulmonary resuscitation (CPR) just in case they have a coronary problem, to keep in close contact with their doctors, and never to exceed their target heart rate (which should be established by a doctor's stress test beforehand).

To be of any good to heart patients (or to anyone, for that matter), exercising can't be temporary. It's got to be a lifetime pact a person makes with himself or herself. Unfortunately, Kate Booth and other cardiac rehabilitation experts have found that roughly 50 percent of patients quit their exercise programs, and many of these patients end up right back in the hospital with another heart attack and then back in a rehabilitation program. Or worse, they end up as a sudden-death statistic. Dr. Roy J. Shephard of the University of Toronto analyzed the data from 1,318 patients who participated in several large studies and found that those who exercised over the four years following their heart attacks had a mortality rate 25 to 35 percent lower than those who didn't exercise. "Exercisers had a combination of fewer recurrent [cardiac] events and fewer fatal outcomes for recurrences," Dr. Shephard states in his report.

The ones who do stick to an exercise program usually make major modifications in other areas of their lives as well, shedding the old philosophies and habits that may have gotten them into trouble in the first place.

Besides the physical benefits of lower heart rate and increased oxygen capacity, work capacity, and stroke volume, exercise has additional value for those with heart problems—an intangible value that many say makes life worth living again. After a heart attack, there are usually feelings of depression, uncertainty, and fear. "It's not so much a heart attack as an ego attack. Something has happened. They're not right. Men feel that their masculinity is in doubt, that their sexual performance is being questioned," comments Kate Booth. "Then you get them in the program, and after a while they feel better about themselves. They have a new zest for life. They see how much they can do even though they've had a heart attack, and they all of a sudden take pride in their bodies."

Pride is one of the most powerful results of a walking program—whether you're following one to prevent heart disease or to recover from it. It's hard to take pride in a body that strains and sputters just getting around the block, in a heart that aches with each beat. But when your body moves easily and swiftly, like a meticulously tuned machine, it gives you self-confidence and lifts your spirits.

Risky Business

Here are the risk factors that the National Institutes of Health have found to be strongly associated with heart disease.

- Cigarette smoking
- High blood pressure
- High blood cholesterol
- Age
- Family history
- Obesity
- Diabetes mellitus
- Physical inactivity
- Behavior patterns

(6)

Walking to Make Your Body Work Better

Your heart isn't the only part of your body that will benefit from walking. Regular walking has been shown to help reduce symptoms of diabetes; osteoporosis; Raynaud's disease; insomnia; back problems; asthma, chronic bronchitis, and emphysema; and certain types of arthritis. In addition, it can improve your sex life and possibly increase your immunities. Many ardent walkers report that walking has cured them of ailments from headache to heartburn. So get going, and find out for yourself all the ways that walking can make *your* body work better!

Diabetes

There are approximately 10 million diabetics in the United States today. According to many experts, these 10 million people could benefit from walking. There are two types of diabetes, classified as Type I and Type II. With Type I diabetes, which occurs most often in children and young adults, little or no insulin is produced by the pancreas; therefore, daily injections of insulin are required to enable the patient to metabolize sugar properly. Insulin allows the body to take glucose from the bloodstream and convert it to fuel for the body. Without proper insulin levels, glucose builds up in the bloodstream and can cause serious complications, such as blindness, kidney damage, and death.

The majority of diabetics—about 8 million of them—have Type II, or non-insulin-dependent diabetes. Type II diabetics usually are able to produce some insulin, but not enough for normal functioning; or, they may produce enough insulin, but their cells are somehow resistant or unable to use it. Type II diabetes usually develops gradually in adulthood, and in many cases it is associated with a substantial weight gain after the age of forty.

One reason for the high incidence of diabetes in people over forty is that the body's ability to properly regulate blood-glucose levels through the release of insulin tends to lessen with age. But, happily, a study published by D. R. Seals and others at the University of Washington School of Medicine in 1984 comparing exercisers and nonexercisers showed that people in their sixties who exercised regularly were able to maintain their glucose tolerance level and insulin sensitivity.

Many doctors think that Type II diabetes in people over forty could be related to physical inactivity and the subsequent increase in body fat, since many people become less active and gain weight as they grow older. Research suggests that, if begun early in life, a sensible diet-and-exercise plan could help prevent the development of Type II diabetes in people with a family history of the disease.

Until recently, treatment for Type II diabetes has mainly been low-fat, low-calorie diets to help patients lose weight. Now many doctors feel that aerobic exercise is equally important in the treatment and prevention of diabetes, and many prescribe walking, since it is easier on the body than other forms of exercise. Exercise helps diabetics because it can dramatically lower blood-sugar levels and actually decrease a diabetic's required insulin dosage. Insulin is still required, but the dose required to keep blood-sugar levels in the normal range is less when the diabetic maintains a regular exercise program.

One reason for this effect is that exercising muscles need more fuel, and thus an active diabetic uses up more glucose. In addition, carbohydrates are used more efficiently. Doctors also suspect that insulin injected into the body gets into the bloodsteam and to the cells that need it more quickly if the diabetic exercises regularly. There is added importance in making walking regular, instead of sporadic. Doctors report that with regular exercise, receptor sites for insulin actually appear to increase in number.

Also vital to diabetics is the role of exercise in reducing the risk of cardiovascular disease, the leading cause of death among diabetics. According to the American Diabetes Association, diabetics are twice as prone to heart disease as non-diabetics. When diabetes is not controlled, patients do not have enough insulin to permit proper use of carbohydrates, so their bodies use fat for energy. This causes the amount of cholesterol and triglycerides in the blood to rise, which contributes to cardiovascular disease. The impaired circulation that results from vascular disease is responsible for increased risk of limb amputation.

If you are a diabetic, you should take some precautions when you exercise. Before you start, consult your physician. It is very important that you undergo an exercise stress test because of the relatively high incidence of undetected cardiovascular disease among diabetics. Also, diabetics may have to increase their walking distances more gradually to prevent heart complications. Both insulin and exercise lower blood-sugar levels, so a new exercise program may also mean that insulin doses need to be adjusted.

After a diabetic has a doctor's green light, he or she might well grab a friend to go along on walks. Doctors advise diabetics not to walk alone, or, if they do, to tell someone where they are going. Diabetics should always carry identification that explains their medical condition and take some form of sugar (sugar water, candy, or sugar cubes, for example) along to guard against the possibility of going into a hypoglycemic state. In addition, they should try to bring along a pocket-sized blood-sugar test, which can be purchased in many pharmacies and quickly can determine blood-glucose levels.

Some diabetics may have a particular problem with dehydration when walking on warm days, so if you are a diabetic, you should drink plenty of fluids and try to walk at the same time each day to better regulate your diet-insulin-exercise program. Also, it's best to walk after, rather than before, meals.

According to Dr. Walter Bortz, a professor of medicine at Stanford University and past president of the American Geriatrics Society, one relatively rare but serious complication of diabetes is neuropathy—near total loss of sensation—in the feet. "While walking won't cure the problem of neuropathy, it does improve circulation, which helps to oxygenate the tissue, which in turn helps to retard some of the nerve loss. And walking is certainly preferable to a jarring activity like jogging," says Bortz. If you have nerve problems in your feet, you should see a podiatrist (foot doctor) and invest in good footware (see chapter 10) to guard against injuries that can lead to infection and more serious complications such as gangrene. And make sure your shoes allow enough room for swelling of your feet, a common problem among diabetics.

Osteoporosis

One of the most conclusive health benefits of walking is its role in the prevention of osteoporosis, a disease associated with the gradual loss of bone tissue with age. Hormonal changes, nutrition, physical activity, and heredity all play roles in the development of osteoporosis, which affects between 10 and 15 million people in the United States including one-fourth of all Caucasian women. The occurrence of osteoporosis is particularly high in postmenopausal women due to a drop in their levels of estrogen, a hormone that helps the body absorb calcium. Some women may lose up to 30 percent of their bone mineral mass by age seventy, according to Dr. Everett L. Smith, director of the biogerontology laboratory at the University of Wisconsin in Madison.

In severe cases of osteoporosis, bones become very fragile and can fracture easily, most commonly in the spine, hips, and wrists. Osteoporosis also leads to poor posture. Weakened bones of the spinal column, compressed by body weight and gravity, can collapse eventually in a crush fracture. Such a collapse can result in decreased height, a humped back, and back pain.

People with osteoporosis are advised to take in more calcium to strengthen their bones (either in their diets or through supplements), and some postmenopausal women are given hormone therapy. However, researchers are finding that these forms of treatment are not enough. "Calcium or hormones alone can't help," says Dr. Charles Gudas, a clinical professor of orthopedic surgery at the University of Chicago. "Exercise is very important. It helps stimulate the absorption of calcium."

One theory suggests that physical activity helps people with osteoporosis because it elevates levels of certain hormones, such as growth and sex hormones, that are known to affect bone. A more common explanation is that exercise increases the flow of blood to the bones. Exercised bones become denser by taking up more calcium and phosphorus from the bloodstream.

But the stress on fragile bones should not be jarring. Vigorous stretching and jumping exercises often do a patient more harm than good, says Dr. Carol E. Goodman of the Ochsner Clinic in New Orleans in a report in *Geriatrics*. "The easiest form of weight-bearing exercise is walking, which is the most commonly recommended exercise," she says. Walking doesn't have the spinal stress or the risk of bone injury associated with most other aerobic exercises.

Over the last five years, extensive research has been conducted to pin down the relationship between exercise and osteoporosis. The results indicate that exercise such as walking helps build vertebral skeletal tissue in both men and women and that people who exercise have more bone density than nonexercisers of the same age.

In a three-year study, Dr. Everett L. Smith and a research team followed a group of women with an average age of eighty-one who exercised three days a week. Their findings showed that the women raised their bone mineral content by 2.29 percent, while a control group who did not exercise lost 3.29 percent over the same time. Another study by B. Krølner and others conducted in Hillerød, Denmark, found that a group of women between the ages of fifty and seventy-three who exercised one hour a day, two days a week, for a period of eighteen months was able to increase the bone mineral content in their spines by 3.5 percent. (A control group of sedentary women lost 2.7 percent.)

Besides walking, women should take additional measures to prevent osteoporosis. Doctors recommend that after menopause, women take in at least 1,500 milligrams each day of calcium with 800 units of vitamin D. To obtain this much calcium, supplements may be necessary, since that's more calcium than you could get by drinking a quart of milk. Also, women need to concentrate on their posture, always sitting and standing as straight as possible.

Raynaud's Disease

If you always seem to get cold feet—even when you're *not* apprehensive—you may have Raynaud's disease, a condition that causes your fingers and toes to become white or blue and extremely stiff and numb in cold weather. It is caused by the constriction of blood vessels in your hands and feet, and it is five times more common in women than in men, according to Dr. Jay Coffman, chief of the peripheral vascular section at Boston University Medical Center.

The numbness or pain in cold weather can be a sign that you have a more serious problem, such as rheumatoid arthritis or scleroderma (a disease causing the skin to harden), but for most people with Raynaud's disease, walking can help. "Walking increases the dilation of blood vessels," explains Dr. Bortz, "so it can greatly decrease the swelling, discoloration, pain, and numbness that plague people with Raynaud's."

Martha Marks, a seventy-five-year-old from New York who suffers from Raynaud's, started walking to help bring down her cholesterol level and to control her weight. After she had walked a few months, the weather started getting cold, and Martha noticed another added benefit: "My hands and feet didn't get as cold as they used to. I wasn't expecting it, but walking actually improved my circulation."

At the same time, walking also helps reduce stress (see

chapter 8), which has been shown to aggravate Raynaud's. If a person is less stressed, he or she is less likely to have regular recurrences of the condition.

Improved Sleep

Many people have some trouble sleeping every once in a while, and about 20 percent of adults have more serious cases of insomnia. People generally have more trouble getting a good night's sleep as they get older.

To combat restless nights, people try everything from over-the-counter drugs to counting sheep. What many people do not realize is that another by-product of walking is sound sleep. When you walk regularly, you will likely see a positive change in your sleeping pattern—as long as walking isn't done late in the evening. Heavy exercise shortly before bedtime can cause your respiration and heart rates to rise and can keep you from relaxing.

Colin M. Shapiro and a research team at the Royal Edinburgh Hospital in Scotland studied a group of army recruits for eighteen weeks and found that the more fit they became, the better they slept—meaning they fell asleep more quickly and woke up less often during the night. Their study also found that as time went on, the men needed less sleep each night to feel rested the next day.

And exercising is a better route to a good night's sleep than drugs because drugs actually can inhibit deep sleep and thus keep you from feeling refreshed in the morning. Many sleeping drugs stay in the bloodstream long after morning, so you may feel foggy all day, and they are habit-forming. Walking brings about sleep naturally by stimulating the secretion of sleep-inducing endorphins, which are brain chemicals that lift your spirits and calm you down. As a result, you will sleep more deeply and soundly. Since walking helps reduce stress, you'll feel less tense, which also helps keep you from staring at the ceiling all night. Some exercisers, including walkers, find that they can't sleep well unless they've worked out that day. If you have trouble sleeping, perhaps you should be counting miles instead of sheep!

Back Problems

Annually in the United States some 7 million persons will experience back problems, according to the National Institutes of Health. Some experts say that 80 percent of all back pain is due to inadequate exercise. So if you want to avoid backaches, one of your best recourses may be to go out and walk.

Most backaches occur because weak abdominal and back muscles cannot support the spine, and, as a result, swayback causes pressure on the sensitive vertebrae in the spine. Regular walking can strengthen abdominal and back muscles. Every time you lift your legs, you're not only using your thighs and calves, but you're also engaging the muscles in the lower abdomen in the process—so they are getting a workout too. With tighter, stronger abdominal muscles, you will stand taller and have less back pain. In addition, when you are in good physical condition, you are less prone to back injuries.

Walking also can help get rid of excess weight, a major cause of back problems, especially when the weight is carried in the stomach. A potbelly can further pull the spine forward and further weaken the abdominal muscles. Reducing a flabby middle can thus improve your posture.

Some back problems are age-related. "Up until about age eighty, all the joints in the body retain very good mobility for usual activities—except the spine," says Dr. Ray Bellamy, an orthopedic surgeon at the Tallahassee (Florida) Memorial Regional Medical Center and the coauthor of a study on the effects of aging on joint mobility. When people are in their thirties, stiffness in the spine often sets in, and as they get older, the loss of flexibility progresses. Walking, in addition to back extension exercises and good posture, can help this problem. "Motion is good for joints; joints need motion," states Dr. Bellamy.

Asthma, Chronic Bronchitis, and Emphysema

Eighteen million Americans suffer from asthma, chronic bronchitis, or emphysema, and the number is rising each year. But there is hope, according to the American Lung Association, and it comes from walking. Smoking and air pollution are the major factors contributing to these lung diseases, which are most common among males between fifty and seventy years of age. These conditions usually come on gradually and are characterized by a bad head cold; a heavy, persistent cough; or shortness of breath.

Walking can help by toning up the muscles of your chest and abdomen. "It has been very clearly demonstrated in individuals with lung ailments that walking makes people—including asthma, bronchitis, and emphysema sufferers—breathe easier," says Dr. Bortz. The correlation between walking and relief from respiratory problems is less a function of the changes in the lung itself and more a strengthening of the surrounding muscles. "The muscles in the chest wall are just like the muscles in your arms and legs," he says. "They need to be strong to control the diaphragm, which makes the work of breathing easier and the exchange of oxygen and carbon dioxide more efficient."

Another reason exercise helps people with respiratory problems is that trained muscles of the body need less oxygen than weak ones; therefore the individual does not have to breathe as hard to take in that oxygen. "Emphysema patients get so out of breath when they walk because their muscles are inefficient for their condition," explains Dr. Robert Sandhaus of the National Asthma Center. "When they do start exercising, they won't necessarily feel 'stronger,' but they'll find that they aren't out of breath so often."

Some asthmatics have attacks that are brought on by strenuous exercise, but as asthma sufferers become better trained, their attacks may occur less frequently, and the severity or duration of the attacks should decrease. Some doctors believe that exercise gives the asthmatic more emotional independence and makes the person more fit and more resistant to attacks.

If you have any respiratory ailments, it is important that you consult a doctor before beginning a walking program. If you are on a medication schedule, it may need to be adjusted to fit in with your new walking regimen.

Arthritis

Too many people with arthritis feel that the best thing they can do for it is nothing at all. When movements hurt, it is natural to try to avoid them. According to the Arthritis Foundation, however, prescribed exercise, along with medication and rest periods, can actually relieve pain and help reverse the inflammation, joint damage, and impaired movement associated with some types of arthritis.

People with certain kinds of mild to moderate arthritis can be helped by walking. Strenuous exercises like jogging and tennis may cause further joint damage, but walking seems to have the opposite effect. Rheumatologists see now a correlation between walking and arthritis benefits. Walking helps stabilize the joints, while keeping them from fixing in one position. Without movement, ligaments and tendons deteriorate. And walking seems to be one of the best, least jarring exercises for keeping the joints in motion. So, if you have arthritis, check with your doctor first, and then get on the road to recovery—with walking.

Improved Sex Life

Some people look in books and magazines. Some try candlelight and soft music. Others resort to mythical aphrodisiacs such as ginseng and oysters. Well, some recent studies suggest that if you are looking to improve your sex life, you should start by looking to your feet. You see, walking, while not the sexiest activity itself, does help in matters of passion.

Exercise such as walking may actually extend the number of years you remain sexually active, according to Dr. James Skinner, director of the Exercise and Sport Research Institute at Arizona State University. One reason behind his theory is that exercise stimulates the release of a wide range of hormones, including some, such as testosterone, that have been shown to contribute to sex drive.

A study of American and Australian male runners showed that after twenty minutes of aerobic exercise, testosterone levels rose sharply. Testosterone is a hormone that helps exercising muscles store energy in the form of glycogen, and it may also speed up the metabolism of carbohydrates in muscles. This leads to increased energy levels, and possibly an increased sex drive. It is still uncertain whether this hormonal change produced by exercise is long-lasting. There is some doubt because the human body adjusts itself to hormonal changes fairly rapidly, soon bringing levels back to normal.

Some doctors believe that strength and cardiovascular improvement from aerobic exercise results in better sexual performance. Sedentary people tend to feel stress about sexual drive and performance, which inhibits them and only leads to more sexual stress and fear. Conversely, people who exercise regularly feel better about their bodies, have less fears about sexual performance, and are able to have sex—or perform any energetic task—for longer periods of time without tiring. In addition, exercise promotes a better body image, and a positive self-image is very important to human sexuality.

Will too much exercise make people too tired for sex? The energy required for the sex, according to Dr. Skinner, is equivalent to the energy needed for walking up two flights of stairs. So sex is no longer thought to be as strenuous as it was once thought. However, orgasmic sex can raise the heart rate of people who are out of shape to 70 percent of their maximum. Once again, walking may be the answer. "If the older or obese person gets into shape, sex will demand only 40 to 50 percent of [his or her] heart-lung potential," reports Skinner.

Increased Immunities

Researchers are finding that regular exercise may actually help the body fight off many kinds of infection. According to Dr. Harvey B. Simon of the Harvard Medical School, several recent studies have shown that levels of certain immunological agents in the body increase with exercise. In the March 1985 issue, *American Health* magazine reports that scientists think that when you exercise, your white blood cells release the same chemical they use when fighting bacteria. "This chemical raises your body temperature, causing a fever in one case and a post-workout glow in the other," the report says. "When you're sick, fever has a purpose: It makes it tough for germs to reproduce. A super-heated athlete's body may fight infection the same way." However, studies on immunology and exercise are still inconclusive.

(7)

Walking to Lose Weight

Sixty pounds overweight at age fifty-one, Lona Rubenstein of East Hampton, New York, decided to "get moving." She had tried a multitude of diets, each one eventually unsuccessful. Then, ten years ago, she turned to walking, going out for thirty-five minutes five times a week. And it has paid off. Over the years, she has lost a total of 100 pounds. "Once I set up a regular routine, the weight loss came naturally," says Rubenstein. "I was less hungry, and I started to learn which foods were best for my energy. Not only am I thinner, but I function better both mentally and physically."

Until 1977, the most exercise fifty-seven-year-old Dr. Rose Caron, a psychology professor at George Washington University, got was standing behind the podium teaching her classes. Then she decided she had to do something about the extra weight she had acquired from doing nothing but standing, so she took up walking. "I didn't want to lose weight for cosmetic reasons, but more for my health. I chose walking over aerobics classes, swimming, and the other exercises because it was practical and simple, and it gave me some time to sort out my thoughts." As a result, she is now fifty pounds slimmer and says she feels more in control of her life than ever.

Lona Rubenstein and Rose Caron aren't the only ones who have discovered the value of walking when it comes to losing weight. Doctors, fitness experts, and many waistline-watchers agree that aerobic exercise is the key factor in controlling that number that registers on the scale in the morning. "Regular exercise can be the single most useful thing a moderately obese person can do to lose weight," says Dr. Joël Grinker, professor of nutrition at the University of Michigan. "I tell almost everyone that walking is the best exercise they can get because it doesn't stress the body the way running does."

This, however, is a relatively new concept. For years trying to lose or control weight meant only one thing—a near starvation diet of rabbit food and bird-sized portions. The whole point was to take in as few calories as possible, and, as a result, a lot of unhappy people tortured themselves at parties, during holidays, and every time they walked by a bakery.

The point now is to *burn* as many calories as possible. It was long believed that the way people got overweight and stayed that way was by eating too much. Some of the latest research, however, suggests that in some cases overweight people do not eat more food than their thinner counterparts. The difference is that they are not as active.

With exercise, some doctors say, many people can eat just as much as they did when they were sedentary and still lose the weight they want to get rid of. You can be at your thinnest—and your healthiest—through walking.

The Problem with Being Overweight

A person is generally considered obese if he or she weighs 20 percent or more above his or her ideal weight. (See the Metropolitan Life Insurance tables on page 93 for desirable weights.) For example, a five-feet, four-inch tall woman with a medium build would be considered obese, according to the tables, if she weighs 165 pounds or more, since the highest end of her desirable weight range is 138 pounds.

Approximately 34 million Americans fit this definition

of obesity. Of these, more than 11 million are severely obese. And despite the fitness boom and the more health-conscious times, more people in the United States are overweight now than a generation ago.

All this extra weight is more than unattractive; it is a potential killer, according to the National Institutes of Health (NIH). People who are overweight are more susceptible to high cholesterol levels in the blood, cancer, heart disease, adult-onset diabetes, gallbladder disease, respiratory problems, and arthritis. "We have found that there are multiple biological hazards at what are surprisingly low levels of obesity," Dr. Jules Hirsch, an obesity researcher at Rockefeller University in New York, told the *New York Times*. Hirsch believes that even people 5 to 10 percent overweight are at greater risk of developing serious health problems. Being even 5 percent above your desirable weight can result in a life span shortened by as much as 5 percent, it was reported at a recent NIH conference.

Extra pounds are a major concern for most everyone, but even more so for older people. With age, many people become less active and, thus, put on weight. There is an age-related decline in lean body mass and a rise in total body fat. In addition, metabolism slows over the years, so even if you eat the same amount of food that you did when you were in your thirties, you won't, if you're like most people, burn it off as quickly. "Each decade of your life, your metabolic rate slows down by 6 percent," says Barbara Ecker, a nutritionist and general manager of technical services for Weight Watchers International. "To lose weight, you have to cut back on your food by 6 percent and/or increase your activity." And one of the two activities recommended by Weight Watchers to its members is walking. The other is stair climbing.

How Exercise Helps You Lose Weight

The secret to losing weight is simply to use more calories than you take in. There are basically two ways in which you can do this. One way is to stop eating as much so that your normal daily activities use up more calories than you consume. Using this method, doctors estimate you can lose about one pound a week. By cutting out 500 calories a day from your diet over a week, you can reduce your intake by 3,500 calories, the number of calories in a pound of fat.

The other way is to exercise and burn off more calories. In a landmark study that debunked the commonly held belief that you have to consume fewer calories to lose weight, Grant Gwinup of the University of California at Irvine showed that obese women could drop pounds by exercising only. The year-long study followed eleven obese women who walked at least thirty minutes a day and stuck to their normal diets. Over the year, they lost an average of twenty-two pounds each. In addition, Dr. Abraham Alfaro of Tri-Fitness, Inc., in New York City, said at the International Conference on Exercise and Aging in July 1985 that physical training can help prevent the age-related decline in lean body mass and the simultaneous increase in body fat.

Doctors estimate that if you start exercising and do not make any changes in your diet, you should be able to lose about one-half pound a week. And if you exercise and modify your diet, you should expect to lose about one and a half pounds per week. You should not have to cut back your caloric intake drastically. Moderation is the answer. Many doctors think that limiting your portion size, reducing your consumption of certain foods, and doing some sort of exercise, such as walking regularly, is the safest, most effective way to lose weight.

Doctors are steering people away from dieting only and including exercise for many reasons. First, you burn 360 to 420 calories per hour when you walk briskly. In addition, evidence indicates that you burn calories even after you *stop* exercising. Following a workout, your basal metabolic rate (BMR) rises. The BMR is a measure of the amount of energy the body uses to maintain its vital function. In a 1960 study, subjects walked ten miles at a rate of four miles per hour. For seven hours after they finished, their BMR was 14 to 18 percent above normal.

On the other hand, when you diet and diet only, your metabolic rate actually slows down. Dr. C. Wayne Callaway, director of the nutrition clinic at the Mayo Clinic in

Calorie Expenditures When Walking at Various Speeds	
Speed (miles per hour)	Calories Burned (per hour)
2	120–150
3	240–300
3 1/2	300–360
4	360–420

Rochester, Minnesota, explains, "Reductions in calorie intake are accompanied by reductions in energy expenditure, an adaptation which allows the individual to survive longer periods of starvation or semistarvation than would otherwise be possible." What this means is that if you merely cut down on your calories, your body is simply going to use fewer calories, and you will have a harder time shedding pounds. This is why you hear so many dieters say things like, "I'm not eating as much, but I haven't lost any weight."

"The body can't tell the difference between the first day in a concentration camp and the first day on a diet," says Dr. Peter D. Wood, a professor of medicine at Stanford University. "In both cases, it tends to react by lowering its metabolic rate, which is, in fact, thwarting the diet."

This decrease in metabolic rate seems to explain why many dieters have trouble keeping their weight below a certain level—a level that has recently been referred to as "set point." Set point is the weight your body seems to hover at (give or take a few pounds) when you aren't dieting or even thinking about what you eat. It is the weight your body will go back up to after a diet has failed. This can be very frustrating for dieters because it makes them feel that they have little control over their weight. Your set point, however, can be changed—not through dieting alone, but through exercise. Proponents of the set point theory seem to think that you cannot get your weight below a certain level because your brain tries to keep a specific ratio of fat to muscle in your body. Once a person begins to exercise, his or her body seems to sense that it must find a new weight level, and a new balance of fat to muscle, in order to sustain the activity.

Another reason it is not a good idea to try to lose weight only by eating less is that you likely will lose the wrong kind of weight. Studies of dieters done by Dr. Arthur Weltman and Dr. Bryant Stamford show that as much as one-third of the weight lost is lean muscle tissue. This is weight you want to keep, especially as you get older and your body is losing muscle tissue already through the aging process. When you exercise, however, you burn off mostly fat and will usually gain lean muscle tissue. Thus, people who regularly exercise to lose weight generally will get rid of more fat and end up with more muscle, which gives them firmer, harder bodies than dieting alone could.

If exercise is so much more effective than mere dieting as a weight-loss tool, why do so many people still try every new diet that comes out? Because most people want to lose weight fast, and most fad diets allow you to do this—temporarily. "Dieting is the most common, most misunderstood, and most abused way of losing weight. Too many of us judge a diet's merit by how quickly it takes off weight," say Weltman and Stamford in an article in *The Physician and Sportsmedicine*. "A fairly pronounced weight loss may occur at the beginning of any diet, because the body's glycogen [starch] stores are depleted and some body water is lost." This initial drop is deceptive, however. There is nothing desirable about losing body water, and nothing healthy about it either. If the water is not replaced, you can become dehydrated, and once you replace the water, as you should, the scale will climb up again. "As you get into the second and third week, you may start regaining some of that water, and your weight actually starts going back up," says Dr. Peter Wood. "It's really frustrating to the dieter, because he's still not eating, but his weight is going up. . . . [This] accounts for the same person trying one diet after the other, desperately searching for one that *will* work."

People who want to lose weight must face the fact that

there is no quick way to do it. Anything quick is probably not good for you. Exercise allows you to stay healthy while losing weight. You shed pounds gradually, just as they were put on, and you don't have to go without good food, since you are burning off additional calories. In fact, Dr. Wood emphasizes, you can probably eat more when you exercise and still lose weight. Dr. Wood tells of many exercisers who saw the numbers on the scale march downward while the amount of food on their plates was increasing. It sounds too good to be true—losing weight without having to give up second helpings or walk across the street when you approach a chocolate-chip cookie shop.

And because you don't have to skimp on food, you can eat better, more balanced meals and thereby get all the vitamins and minerals you need. Many dieters sacrifice good nutrition when they cut down on their eating—unwise at any age, but particularly so as you get older.

In addition, when you walk to lose weight, you get all the health benefits that go along with exercise, such as added protection from heart disease and diabetes. There are no added health benefits in starving yourself, just health risks. Extreme dieting may bring about such symptoms as low tolerance of cold temperatures, dry skin and hair, constipation, difficulty in concentrating, and mood changes.

The Gwinup study mentioned earlier found that subjects lost weight without any of the adverse effects often associated with dieting. "[The subjects] frequently commented that weight loss through exercise, unlike that previously achieved through dieting, was not accompanied by feelings of weakness and increased nervousness, but rather by feelings of increased strength and relaxation," the author reports.

Without these drawbacks, without the hunger pangs that come with dieting, it is easier to stick to a long-term weight-loss plan. Many people abandon diets out of frustration because the diets are too restricting. Some dieters have to eat carrot sticks at parties instead of delicious-looking hors d'oeuvres. They have to order the plain broiled fish at a restaurant instead of the lasagna they would really like. Every day their willpower is put to the test. Many who fail the test give up and go back to their old eating habits, and, usually, their old weight.

When you exercise, you have more freedom with what you eat. Of course, you should not think you can eat an ice-cream sundae every day just because you walk regularly. But you can eat more of the foods you love when you walk without worrying that the scale will take a jump toward catastrophe. As long as you generally stick to a sensible, well-balanced diet, you should be able to burn off the calories you take in—even those from an occasional treat. Besides, if you do go on a binge or really overdo at a party, you can walk a little farther for a few days to make up for it. The secret is flexibility; the more flexible a weight-loss plan is, the better chance you will stay with it on a long-term basis.

"There have been studies showing that for people who lose weight successfully and keep it off, one of the key factors is that they weave exercise into their lifestyle," says Barbara Ecker of Weight Watchers International. "And the trick, after all, is not to lose weight, but to lose it and keep it off. Exercise can make the difference."

Another advantage of walking is that it reduces the nervous stress (see chapter 8) that causes some people to eat compulsively. "In a test we did with our members," says Ecker, "one of the side benefits was release of nervous tension." Ida Green, sixty-nine, of San Francisco is one person who has stopped her nervous snacking thanks to her walking program. "Whenever I was depressed or upset, I'd reach for a doughnut, candy, or ice cream—anything I could get my hands on. Sometimes I would eat half a cake without realizing it," she says. "But since I've started walking, I really don't get as nervous, and when I do, I go outside and walk some instead of going to the refrigerator." Over the past year, Ida has lost twenty pounds.

For walking truly to be effective in losing weight, you should go out for thirty minutes at least four times a week. "People who exercised four or five times a week lost weight three times faster than those who only exercised three days a week, and one or two sessions were ineffective," say Dr. William Bennett and Joel Gurin in their book, *The Dieter's*

Dilemma: Eating Less and Weighing More. In addition, it seems that the best time to exercise to lose weight may be early in the morning, according to the Institute for Aerobics Research in Dallas. This may be because your body will have to use stored-up energy if you work out twelve hours after you have last eaten.

But whenever you exercise, just try to make it part of your lifestyle and stick with it. Then, reap the rewards—and the compliments. Marcia Coltren, a retiree from Manhattan, has lost fifteen pounds in one year through her walking. "I feel better now that I'm thinner," she says. "I feel better all over."

Food for Energy

When you start walking, you will probably find that you need more energy than you used to, since you will be burning up much more of it. You can get that extra energy by eating the right foods.

Many nutritionists think that the key to eating for energy lies in complex carbohydrates, including breads, cereals, potatoes, rice, pasta, and other starches. People generally think of these foods as diet no-nos, but the toppings and all the extras put on such items are the true culprits, not the foods themselves. Complex carbohydrates are very good for you, especially when you are exercising. Carbohydrates are stored in the muscles in the form of glycogen, which is muscle sugar, and glycogen is what fuels the muscles. That's why you hear about runners and other athletes eating pasta before an event. What works for them can work for you.

Fruit is also a good high-energy food because it has both complex carbohydrates (starches) and simple carbohydrates (sugars). It is good to avoid foods that are all, or mainly, sugar.

One of the best ways to maintain your energy level is to drink plenty of water. Without enough water, you can become dehydrated, and this will impair your performance.

Food to Walk Away From

You should avoid some types of food no matter how hard you are exercising. This includes foods high in cholesterol, salt, and sugar.

Foods high in cholesterol. Many Americans were practically raised on eggs and bacon, thick steaks, butter, and cream. Ironically, such foods were once considered healthy and nutritious. Today, however, it has been determined that these foods should be consumed with moderation and caution. The American Heart Association recommends that no more than 30 percent of your daily calorie consumption come from fats. However, the diet for most Americans is more than 40 percent fat. The AHA also suggests that the intake of cholesterol be reduced to 250 to 300 milligrams a day (one egg contains about 275 milligrams of cholesterol). To be safe, you should try to keep your cholesterol level under 200 milligrams per deciliter of blood.

Although a certain amount of cholesterol is vital to bodily functions, too many people eat too many fried foods and too many products derived from animals, such as cuts of meat, eggs, and butter. When you eat an excessive amount of saturated fats, not only do you add to your total body fat, but you also increase your chances of developing coronary heart disease. As discussed in chapter five, high levels of cholesterol in the blood can lead to atherosclerosis, in which fatty deposits form inside the arteries and interfere with the flow of blood. If a coronary artery is blocked, the result is a heart attack.

The American Heart Association suggests that you have no more than three egg yolks per week, that you limit your consumption of shrimp and organ meats, and that you eat no more than six ounces of meat, fish, or poultry per day. Instead of frying foods, try boiling, steaming, or baking them. Substitute margarine for butter, and instead of whole milk or cheese made from whole milk, use skimmed or low-fat milk and cheese made from partially skimmed milk.

Foods high in salt. Nutritionists say that Americans generally consume twice as much sodium—in the form of salt—as they need. About 1,100 to 3,300 milligrams of sodium a day is adequate; however, the average consumption is 5,000 milligrams per day. It is easy to take in too much salt, even if you personally don't ever turn over the shaker, because many foods have quite a bit of salt added for taste and as a preservative. A high-sodium diet is known to cause hypertension, which eventually can lead to heart attack, stroke, and kidney disease. Sodium is a nutrient that helps regulate water balance in the body. When consumed in excess, it can cause fluid retention, which will make you feel bloated.

You can reduce your intake of sodium by using herbs to season food instead of salt. You may miss salt at first, but you will probably be surprised at how quickly you can adjust to the taste of food without it. In addition, there are many low-salt products and salt substitutes on the market that make the going easier.

Foods high in sugar. Researchers say that the dramatic rise in heart attacks in the United States largely has been related to the increase in sugar and fat consumption. Sugar is the ultimate junk food. It has a false reputation for boosting energy; it decays teeth; and, of course, it puts on pounds. What's worse is that sugar is not only found in candy, ice cream, and cake, but it also is hidden in products that you wouldn't expect contained sugar, such as salad dressing, vegetable juices, and some soups.

When you consume too much sugar, it increases the glucose level in your blood and stimulates the pancreas to secrete insulin. This hormone, which controls the level of the body's blood sugar, is manufactured in the pancreas. Such stimulation can cause the pancreas to produce excess insulin; in the short term, this causes the blood sugar to plummet. A person can, as a result, suffer symptoms of low blood sugar, or hypoglycemia. In a hypoglycemic state, you will crave sweets to boost your blood-sugar level. This is why it is so difficult to eat just a few sweets and why sugar binges are common.

As you get older, the pancreas does not produce as much insulin. This compounds the danger of taking in too much sugar. Your best bet for avoiding the problem of diabetes is to eat as little sugar as possible and still maintain a balanced diet. Use sugar substitutes when you can, and read the labels of products to check for hidden sugar.

Figuring Your Desirable Weight

To determine how much you should weigh ideally, you could simply check the charts that follow; for a more specific figure, you can use the formula below.

Women should allow 100 pounds for their first five feet of height and an additional five pounds for every inch above that. Men should figure on 106 pounds for their first five feet plus six pounds for every additional inch. You will also have to take into account your body build. The size of your wrists will tell you whether you have a small, average, or large build. Wrap your middle finger and thumb around your wrist. If they barely touch, you probably have an average build; if so, the figure you arrived at above is your ideal weight. If your fingers overlap, your frame is small. Subtract 10 percent from the figure you calculated above for your ideal weight. If your fingers don't touch, you have a large frame. Add 10 pecent to the figure you arrived at above to determine your ideal weight.

On the following page are the most recent Metropolitan Life Insurance Company weight tables for suggested weight ranges by height and size of frame (determine your frame size as directed above) for people weighed barefoot and without clothing. *These are suggested weight ranges only.*

MEN

Height	Small Frame	Medium Frame	Large Frame
5'1"	123–129	126–136	133–145
5'2"	125–131	128–138	135–148
5'3"	127–133	130–140	137–151
5'4"	129–135	132–143	139–155
5'5"	131–137	134–146	141–159
5'6"	133–140	137–149	144–163
5'7"	135–143	140–152	147–167
5'8"	137–146	143–155	150–171
5'9"	139–149	146–158	153–175
5'10"	141–152	149–161	156–179
5'11"	144–155	152–165	159–183
6'0"	147–159	155–169	163–187
6'1"	150–163	159–173	167–192
6'2"	153–167	162–177	171–197
6'3"	157–171	166–182	176–202

WOMEN

Height	Small Frame	Medium Frame	Large Frame
4'9"	99–108	106–118	115–128
4'10"	100–110	108–120	117–131
4'11"	101–112	110–123	119–134
5'0"	103–115	112–126	122–137
5'1"	105–118	115–129	125–140
5'2"	108–121	118–132	128–144
5'3"	111–124	121–135	131–148
5'4"	114–127	124–138	134–152
5'5"	117–130	127–141	137–156
5'6"	120–133	130–144	140–160
5'7"	123–136	133–147	143–164
5'8"	126–139	136–150	146–167
5'9"	129–142	139–153	149–170
5'10"	132–145	142–156	152–173

(8)

Walking to Reduce Stress

It's early in the morning. You are on your way to a shopping trip downtown. When you go to start your car, all you hear is a "cough, cough, clunk." When you try again, you hear nothing. You try to stay calm and decide to take the bus instead.

You are waiting at the bus stop. Ten minutes pass. Then twenty. Then thirty. Finally, forty minutes after its scheduled arrival, the bus approaches, but it is so packed you can't get on. You clench your fists and feel your heart pounding in your chest. You give up on your trip into town and walk to the corner supermarket to purchase a few items.

As you pick up your bag of groceries to leave the store, the bottom tears open. A bottle breaks on the floor, and ketchup splatters all over your new slacks. The muscles in your neck tense as you wonder to yourself why this is happening to you.

Then, to add insult to injury, when you get back home and open your mail, you find a notice that says the last check you wrote bounced. "That's it," you say, and head for your bedroom to take a nap to try to relieve your tension. Just as you lay your throbbing head back, the neighbor's dog begins barking . . . and barking . . . and barking . . .

Life's daily hassles—minor if considered individually, but collectively they're enough to make a person think that being marooned on a desert island might not be so bad. But you don't have to go that far to reduce the tension caused by the little problems that pick at you like so many mosquitoes; often you need only go around the neighborhood or the park—on a walk! Yes, you can add "stress reliever" to the growing list of the benefits of walking. Exercise, and specifically walking, can take the bite out of life's stressors—the small kind just mentioned as well as the big ones, such as an unsatisfying job, adjusting to retirement, or even the death of a loved one.

"Anxiety and depression are common symptoms of failure to cope with mental stress, and exercise has been associated with a decreased level of mild to moderate depression and anxiety." This was one of the findings of a conference dealing with exercise and mental health sponsored by the National Institute of Mental Health in 1984.

To understand *how* exercise reduces stress, it is important to know what stress does to your body in the first place.

Your Body's Reaction to Stress

Everyone feels it at some point or another—the tightening of the muscles, the acceleration of the heartbeat, the quickening of the breath. These are all symptoms of stress, but despite the bad press stress has gotten lately, not all forms of stress are harmful. There is positive stress and negative stress. Positive stress is a temporary surge of adrenaline and tension that comes, say, when you are walking down a dark street and you hear footsteps behind you. Your body is getting revved up for a sudden "fight or flight." Also, if you are preparing to make a presentation to the boss, the anxiety you feel helps you get primed for the task.

On the other hand, stress can make you a physical mess if you react to even minor snafus with tense muscles and faster heartbeat; if you are constantly in this hyped-up, geared-up state; or if it becomes a way of life. Continuous stress can cause you to become unproductive, irritable, short-tempered, easily frustrated, or depressed—all of which does your health no good. According to the American Academy of Family Physicians, two-thirds of all visits to family doctors are prompted by stress-related symptoms. The range of health problems that have been linked to stress is wide—from migraine headaches to multiple sclerosis, from diabetes to genital herpes. And, most frightening, stress is now known to be a major contributor, either directly or indirectly, to six of the biggest killers in the country: cancer, lung disease, cirrhosis of the liver, accidents, heart disease, and suicide.

One explanation for the devastating effect of chronic stress on the body comes from a study by Steven Schleifer and researchers at the Mount Sinai Medical Center in New York. They found that stress weakens your immune system, leaving you more vulnerable to disease. It causes your heart rate to rise, your blood vessels to constrict (which leads to higher blood pressure), and your blood to thicken. The latter two reactions are believed to be safeguards that evolved to prevent a person wounded during a confrontation from losing a great deal of blood. This was especially useful centuries ago, when humans regularly had to fight for food, land, and dominance. In modern times, however, this clogging that once was so vital in saving lives may have the opposite effect by causing heart disease in people who are constantly feeling stressed.

Even though people often imagine that life after retirement from work will be peaceful and free of the stress that piles up in a hectic workday, many retirees feel a different kind of stress that can be just as debilitating. "Aging, like any other stage of life, has its particular difficulties," says William Rosenblatt, clinical director of the Biofeedback and Stress Management Center in Morristown, New Jersey. "If you used to be able to do something and can't do it now, it can be very stressful unless you determine an effective coping strategy."

Older people are subject to a variety of stressful life changes, including loss of work, reduced income, the deaths of friends, and illness or death of a spouse.

Walking seems to be particularly effective in reducing

the depression that sometimes comes with these life changes. Several studies have demonstrated improvements in persons who began exercising after retirement even though they had never exercised previously. David C. Morris, a sociologist at Ball State University in Indiana, has found that participation in sports activities is a key variable that directly affects a retired person's satisfaction with life.

As people get older, they are more likely to feel stress about their health and the decline in their physical abilities. All of this makes exercise even more important for older people; it improves physical health, which can ease the anxiety about the age-related decline in fitness and, thus, lead to better *psychological* health.

How Walking Reduces Stress

In this high-paced, high-anxiety world, it is important to find a positive plan for coping with the strains of life. Many people turn to alcohol, drugs, and cigarettes, which are not only expensive monetarily, but health-wise as well. One of the healthiest, cheapest, most productive ways you can chase stress away is on foot. Here are eight reasons:

1. Your body wants to move. Have you ever come home at the end of a stressful day and had the urge to lash out at something, such as a punching bag? That is because stress has caused your body to prepare for a physical challenge (fight) or escape (flight), and often you need to take physical action to release the tension. "Meditation techniques and breathing exercises are helpful in terms of prevention and attempting to manage part of the stressful situation. But when the adrenaline is pumping through the veins, the only real way to get rid of it is to use the body, to do what it is geared up to do at that point, which is take some exercise and exhaust some of the energy," says William Rosenblatt. "The body is ready for fight or flight, and walking is one of the closest approximations of fleeing that one can get involved in on a regular basis."

"By moving your muscles [when you are under stress], you use up fuel in the blood, reduce your . . . blood pressure, and reverse all the rest of the physiological changes as well," according to Herbert M. Greenberg in *Coping with Job Stress*. His number one recommended muscle mover? "Walking, of course."

2. Exercise produces a high. "Nature's Valium" is what some walkers call their favorite sports activity. "A tranquilizer effect" is what many doctors say exercise can bring about. Exercisers everywhere talk about how a mountain of a problem can look like a molehill after a good workout. The mood-enhancing results of exercise have been well documented, and the most common explanation for this effect (though a direct cause-and-effect relationship has yet to be found) is that during physical activity chemical changes occur in the body. Specifically, there is an increase of certain neurotransmitters (or brain chemicals) that produce a euphoric feeling. "Exercise does seem to raise the level of the three main neurotransmitters—noradrenalin, serotonin, and endorphins," reports Dr. Edward Colt, an endocrinologist in private practice in Manhattan who has studied the effects of exercise on brain chemicals. Endorphins, in particular, are thought to play an important part in making your outlook sunnier; they are called natural opiates.

3. Regular breathing helps reduce tension. Proper breathing not only will help your exercising body to be more efficient, but it will also help ease tension. Be sure to use the breathing techniques described in chapter 4. Deep breathing is a technique commonly taught in stress-management courses. One of the body's responses to stress is rapid, shallow breathing. Breathing slowly and deeply is one of the ways you can shut off your stress reaction and turn on your relaxation response. "If you walk rapidly, your breathing becomes regular, and in this way walking is very similar to meditation, which involves regular breathing," says Dr. Shae Graham Kosch, a psychologist at the University of Florida. "Anything repetitive physically can relieve tension." In addition, taking deep breaths will circulate more oxygen through your body and to your brain, which generally results in a lifting of the spirits.

4. Your circulation improves. When you are under pressure, your surface blood vessels constrict, leaving your hands cold. During exercise, your blood vessels dilate to accommodate the greater amount of blood the muscles need to do the work. Enlarged blood vessels mean lower blood pressure and generally are associated with more supple and relaxed muscles.

5. Distraction reduces tension. "Walking out in some nice scenery is a marvelous way to get away from thoughts about your business, about the terrible headlines you read in the paper, about whether or not there's going to be a nuclear war," says John Williams, seventy-two, of Largo, Florida. What Williams is reporting is referred to in the scientific world as the distraction theory, which proposes that diversion from stressful stimuli plays a crucial role in reducing tension. "Change is a good rest," says Dr. Colt. "It helps to take time out from the unpleasant aspects of the day."

While some people may find it beneficial to think over their problems while they exercise, William Rosenblatt and other stress experts say it is more productive to empty your mind of your concerns and enjoy the activity. "It is probably much more effective to take a break and relax the mind for a while and forget about your problem," explains Rosenblatt. "Then you'll probably be more effective at solving the problem when you return to it."

Walking, in particular, is a good exercise for stress reduction, Rosenblatt believes, because it is so easy to do and your mind is free to wander. "In terms of adapting to stress, people generally need to start off with an exercise that isn't going to require too many changes or too much effort."

6. Walking outside fights anxiety. You can get rid of tension just by getting outside—away from the fluorescent lights, recirculated air, insulated rooms, blank walls—and into the sunshine, the fresh air, and some natural scenery, (or man-made scenery if you walk in a city). Researchers believe that light, sunlight specifically, may have a tonic effect on the brain and on the body's immune system as well.

And who hasn't felt a little lighter, a little freer, when a nice breeze blows across the face? Who hasn't been lifted by a picturesque scene? Henry David Thoreau certainly knew the value of strolling in the great outdoors. In *Excursions,* he wrote, "I think that I cannot preserve my health and spirits, unless I spend four hours a day at least—and it is commonly more than that—sauntering through the woods and over the hills and fields."

"Instead of sitting around and fretting over your problems or feeling depressed, you have to get out and do something antithetical to anxiety—something that competes with the anxiety response," says Dr. Kosch. "Being out in nature and beautiful scenery is certainly antithetical to being in your room wringing your hands."

7. You gain a sense of mastery. Taxes rise. Companies lay off thousands of workers because of "hard times." The neighborhood store is robbed. A developer decides to build a huge shopping center next to your house or apartment complex. There are many such situations in life that seem beyond your control, and the resulting feelings of helplessness easily can send you spiraling into depression. This leads to other reasons exercise is so effective at beating stress: When you exercise, you feel as if you have more mastery over your own body. You are taking your health into your own hands. You are taking positive action to make your life better.

"If I were to decide to walk, say, half an hour a day, the fact that I am able to stick to it makes me feel good about myself at the beginning," says Rosenblatt. "Then later when I see that I can walk a mile easily when I couldn't do it before, I feel even better about myself. Then I start to think if I can control my fitness, perhaps I have a little more control over my external environment than I thought."

8. You improve your self-concept. This sense of mastery plus a sense of accomplishment and the better body image that you will likely develop once you start getting in shape add up to an improved self-concept. Stressful events have a much greater impact on people with low self-esteem, who seem to take even minor problems much more personally. And older people are susceptible to negative labeling by society simply because they are old, which leads eventually to negative self-labeling as well. Older people must concentrate on keeping a positive self-image to counter this problem. This is where physical activity comes in. "Individuals who exercise and out-perform their sedentary friends are likely to have a higher sense of self-esteem," reports Dr. Bryant Stamford.

If you are feeling snowed under by a pile of pressures, if the day hasn't been going well, or if you just found out about a friend's illness, you can do something about it—right now. The mood-elevating effect of exercise is often immediate; you don't have to walk for weeks or months to feel the benefits.

So, what are you waiting for?

Eight Danger Signs of Stress

Here are eight physical signals that warn that your body's response to stress is becoming destructive. By recognizing these signs, you can learn to change your response to daily tension before it becomes dangerous.

1. Chronic joint pain—muscle spasms or a soreness and tightness in the jaw, back of the neck, shoulders, or lower back.

2. Frequent indigestion, diarrhea, or urination, which can lead to more serious illness such as ulcers or colitis.

3. Susceptibility to colds and viruses. This could be a sign that stress is weakening your immune system.

4. Cold hands, particularly if one hand is colder than the other.

5. Shortness of breath.

6. Sudden proneness to accidents.

7. Headaches and tiredness.

8. Irritability or an inability to share feelings or to feel affectionate and loving.

Walk Out of Depression

Chronic stress can lead to depression unless you learn to cope with pressures and problems. Not only is exercise a preventive medicine for depression, but it can pull people out of "the blues" as well—for many of the same reasons it helps reduce stress. A recent study by I. Lisa McCann and David S. Holmes, psychologists at the University of Kansas, showed that mildly depressed people who exercised were significantly less depressed after ten weeks than people who practiced relaxation techniques or those who did nothing to improve their conditions. An earlier study conducted by John Griest at the University of Wisconsin Medical school and a team of researchers came to a similar conclusion. After twelve weeks of aerobic exercise, mildly depressed subjects showed a reduction in depression, and the improvement was superior to the improvement shown with one form of traditional psychotherapy and equal to that shown with another form of antidepressant therapy. In addition, in a twelve-month follow-up, all but one of the patients were free of symptoms of depression.

One reason those findings are important, says Dr. William Morgan, director of the Sport Psychology Laboratory at the University of Wisconsin–Madison, is that exercise therapy is less expensive than psychotherapy and drugs. In addition, because the condition of moderately depressed people is often worsened by drugs, exercise may offer a non-pharmacologic alternative for treating mild depression.

"I recommend brisk walking—rapid enough to condition the heart—for all my patients who are depressed," says Dr. Ralph Wharton, a New York psychiatrist who specializes in treating depression. "Even twenty to thirty minutes a day seems to make a difference. For one thing going for a walk prevents excessive preoccupation, and rumination, and it distracts you from your own inner concerns—after all, you have to look where you're going!''

How Much Stress Are You Under?

Here is a stress test devised by stress expert Janai Lowenstein of the Conscious Living Foundation in Drain, Oregon, that will give you an idea of whether you need help coping with problems and pressures. Answer each statement with a number value one through five, with each number representing the following:

Never = 1   Rarely = 2   Sometimes = 3   Frequently = 4 Always = 5

1. If plans change at the last minute, I get upset. _____

2. If I forget to buy an item at the store when shopping, I get very tense. _____

3. If I am caught in a traffic jam, anxiety builds inside of me. _____

4. As conditions in my environment become more stressful, I panic and have trouble doing anything. _____

5. When things don't fall nicely into place, I tend to blame others. _____

6. If someone disagrees with my opinion, I get agitated. _____

7. If I have to wait in line ten minutes or more, I lose my temper. _____

8. When I don't fulfill my self-expectations, I get angry at myself. _____

9. I try to do two or more things at once. _____

10. When I get angry, I stay angry for a long time. _____

11. I tend to push my body too hard when I am under pressure. _____

12. I worry about things I cannot control. _____

13. If I am upset, I keep my problems to myself. _____

14. I find retirement (or think it will be) tedious. _____

15. I don't seem to get around to doing the things I would really like to do. _____

Add up the values of your answers, and use this key to find out what your total means.

Total Points

15–30	Low stress level (but there is no harm in taking up walking to make sure stress stays under control).
31–45	Moderate stress level. Walking is suggested to help ease the pressure you feel.
46–60	High stress level. Walking is strongly recommended.
61–75	Excessive stress. Get out on a walking route as soon as possible; you may also want to consult a stress expert for professional therapy.

Tension Busters to Do While Walking

Janai Lowenstein suggests seven ways to enhance the stress-reducing value of walking:

1. Breathe evenly and deeply. Pace your steps evenly with your breathing rate. For example, take four steps while inhaling, four steps while exhaling slowly. The pace will change if you walk more briskly or uphill. By focusing your attention on your breathing, you can clear the mind of stressful thoughts, and the rhythmic pattern is relaxing.

2. Tense and relax your muscles. Most people are unaware of the buildup of muscle tension over the course of a hectic day. To get rid of it, tense one body part while you walk, hold it over a certain number of steps, depending on your pace, and then release the tension while exhaling slowly. Start with your face, and proceed down through your neck, shoulders, arms, hands, chest, stomach, back, buttocks, thighs, and calves.

3. Talk to yourself in self-directed phrases. By talking to yourself while tensing and releasing your muscles, you can enhance the effect. Here are some phrases that will help calm you.

My forehead feels calm and relaxed.

My eyes (cheeks, jaws) are letting tension go.

The muscles in my neck are releasing tension. Continue similarly as you proceed down the body.

4. Use imagery constructively. With each breath, imagine that you are taking in fresh oxygen in the form of white light. As the air enters your body, picture your chest lighting up, then your trunk, then your extremities. Imagine that every part of your body is being lit by the fresh air and that the dark shadows of stress are being wiped out.

5. Get relief from eyestrain. If you spend a lot of time indoors, your eyes get used to working at short distances and in unnatural light. As you begin walking, focus on the ground several feet in front of you. Then, after several minutes, focus on the treetops immediately ahead (you will, of course, have to look down at the ground every once in a while so that you don't stumble). After several more minutes, look to the horizon. Changing your focus often helps relieve eyestrain and tension.

6. Practice self-affirmation. Boost your confidence and self-esteem while you walk by reminding yourself of your value. "I am a good person," tell yourself, repeating as you walk along, "I have a lot to offer."

7. Warm your hands. Cold hands indicate tension; warm hands, calmness. If you are under stress, raising the temperature of your hands increases circulation throughout your body and can help you relax. Check the temperature of your hands by holding them against your neck, which is almost always warm. Here is what you can do to raise your hand temperature: Keep your hands hanging loose at your sides, not in your pockets or crossed in front of you. Say to yourself several times, "My hands are warm and relaxed. I can feel the blood flowing down my arms into my hands." Imagine your hands actually getting warmer. For most people, this will be enough actually to raise the temperature of the hands.

For more information on stress reduction, you can write Janai Lowenstein at the Conscious Living Foundation, PO Box 9, Drain, Oregon 97435.

(9)

Those Little Aches and Pains

Although walking is relatively injury-free, a few aches now and then are almost inevitable, especially if you are starting on an exercise program after years of being sedentary. You will be using muscles that may not have had a good workout in a long while, so it may be a slow, creaky start.

To prevent injuries, keep four general guidelines in mind: First, invest in good shoes with plenty of support and cushion (see chapter 10). Your feet will pay if you get cheap or badly made shoes. Second, always warm up properly before you go out on a walk. If your muscles, tendons, and ligaments are warm and supple, you are less likely to develop any aches than if they are cold. Third, don't try to do more than your body can handle. Many injuries result from trying to progress in an exercise regimen too quickly. Proceed gradually, only stepping up your speed, distance, or frequency after your body has become comfortable with your current level. Last, be aware that proper foot care will go a long way to making your walking injury-free.

Four out of five adults experience foot problems at one time or another. Many of these problems likely could be prevented if everyone spent a few minutes a day checking his or her feet for signs of trouble. And especially as your feet get older, you should pay more attention to them.

How the Foot Ages

Joints and tendons tend to lose their mobility and flexibility over time. "Joint mobility in adults begins a slow decline after the third decade and rapidly declines after the eighth decade," says Dr. Ray Bellamy, an orthopedic surgeon at the Tallahassee Memorial Regional Medical Center.

Biomechanical changes such as bunions and hammer-toes can limit the range of movement of the foot, and the joint spaces in the feet begin to narrow in older people, which means that the joints themselves start to fuse. This is often the onset of osteoarthritis. An X ray of the "older" foot will show a loss of minerals in the bones, with the bones thinner than those in a "younger" foot. The ligaments in the foot will begin to deteriorate and the arch to sag. This is due, in large measure, to the everyday striking, pounding, and stretching that the foot endures over decades (in fact, by the time many people reach fifty-five years of age, they have already walked more than 70,000 miles). Other causes of deteriorated ligaments include biomechanical problems and ill-fitting shoes.

In addition, the older foot loses much of its natural protection against everyday stress and strain. "Through life, fat pads on the bottom of the foot effectively offer natural shock absorption from hard surfaces," explains Dr. Charles Gudas, a clinical professor of orthopedic surgery at the University of Chicago. "In my elderly patients, these fat pads may begin to wear thin so that the built-in protection and padding is diminished. As a result, the foot, especially the heel bone, is more susceptible to shock."

I hope your walking is absolutely pain-free, and, with proper care, it can be. But, just in case, here is a guide to the cause of some of the aches and pains (most relatively minor) you are most likely to develop—if you develop any at all—and how to prevent and treat them.

Corns

Corns are dead skin cells that build up in an area of friction. They can result from improper fit of shoes, tight stockings, hammertoes, or a mechanical imbalance in the structure of the foot. Corns appear on the tips and tops of the toes and between the toes and are very painful when they become inflamed. One kind of corn, a "soft" corn, accumulates moisture, especially between the toes. This type of corn, which usually develops between the fourth and fifth toe, is a source of infection if left untreated, which is one good reason you should examine your feet regularly to find any newly developed corns. If corns are a chronic problem, your doctor may want to perform minor surgery to remove them.

To treat corns, Dr. Suzanne Levine, a New York podiatrist, recommends soaking feet daily (preferably in the morning) in warm, soapy water and then applying a softening or moisturizing cream or petroleum jelly. Then you may want to scrub the surface of the corns with a pumice stone or emery board to prevent the skin from thickening. Most doctors advise against over-the-counter corn drops because the liquid is an acid and may cause burns to the skin and debilitation.

Since corns are often caused by shoes that are too short, narrow, or high in the heel, you may want to try a new pair of shoes or a different shoe size if you have a persistent corn problem. If new shoes don't do the trick, place strips of moleskin (which can be purchased at most pharmacies) on the corns to reduce the friction between your shoes (including your street shoes) and your skin. For soft corns, separate the toes with lambs wool, and keep the area dry with powder. Be sure to wear cotton socks or stockings to absorb perspiration. (If you walk a good deal and your feet perspire accordingly, however, cotton socks may become saturated and hold the moisture next to your skin. If this is the case, some synthetic fabrics may be better for you.)

Calluses

Calluses develop on the bottom of the foot to protect the foot at friction points. One difference from corns is that calluses cover larger areas. Calluses often indicate that your weight is distributed incorrectly on your feet. Calluses can thicken and dig through the skin, causing ulceration. Soak and rub calluses as directed above for corns.

You may think that corns and calluses are not worth worrying about, since they are only dead skin. However, ulceration is a serious condition, and a corn or callus occasionally may irritate a bursal sac around a foot joint and lead to bursitis, a very painful condition. Don't take any risks; attend to corns and calluses carefully.

Blisters

Blisters are caused by heat burns produced by friction between the foot and the shoe. Friction burns and separates the layers of skin, which gradually fill with fluid from tissue cells, forming blisters. If not attended to, blisters can become infected.

Ill-fitting shoes are one of the most common causes of blisters. If your shoes are too small, you will develop blisters on your toes and heels. If your shoes are too big, your feet will slide around and could blister anywhere, but particularly on the front of the foot. Make sure your shoes are the proper size. Check, especially, the toe box (the front part of the shoe that covers the toes). To avoid blisters, it is also important to break in new shoes before embarking on long walks.

Blisters can also be caused by excessive moisture. (Of course, it is best not to get your feet wet when walking in rain or snow.) To prevent this, wear absorbent socks (make sure they are clean and dry). Those made from natural fibers, such as wool or cotton, are preferable. If, however, you find that your socks become saturated on your walks, you might try a pair made from synthetic fibers that are not absorbent. Socks that are cross-woven are recommended because they are more absorbent. Some doctors also recommend wearing two pairs of thin socks rather than one thick pair. Just make sure you at least wear one pair, however. Going without socks is one of the quickest ways to develop a blister.

If you do get a blister, wash it with soap and lukewarm water. Then apply petroleum jelly or powder. Tape gauze over the blister while wearing shoes, but leave it exposed as much as possible to speed healing. If it doesn't heal in twenty-four hours, you may want to have it drained to relieve the pressure you feel when walking on it. It is best to have this done by your physician or podiatrist to be sure that no bacteria are present on the needle or on the skin. For blisters on the heel, you may want to get some kind of padding for your shoe and cut a hole out so as not to irritate the blistered area.

Bunions

Contrary to myth, bunions do not start with ill-fitting shoes. Shoes aggravate bunions; they don't cause them.

Bunions are inherited and tend to grow larger and faster if you wear shoes that are too narrow or pointed. Some people with bunions suffer from lax ligaments. The arch of the foot sags, the ligaments start to spread, and the big toe turns toward the other toes, causing the joint to protrude from the side of the foot. Friction between the protruding joint and the shoe causes swelling of the bursal sac overlying the joint of the big toe. (In certain cases, joint disease can cause bunions. Sometimes bunions are the first sign of rheumatoid arthritis.)

For bunion sufferers, soaking the foot regularly and using pads to protect the joint and to separate the toes may help. Look for shoes that have a wide toe area, or have your shoes stretched in that area. If your bunions are particularly painful or if they keep you from following a walking program, you may want to consider surgery. There are more than a hundred surgical procedures to correct bunions, so research your options carefully. Consult with your podiatrist or orthopedist, and be sure to get a second opinion.

Often what a person thinks is a bunion is, in fact, a condition called hallux limitus, one of the most common hindrances to pain-free walking. In people with this condition, X rays show a noticeable increase in bone mass where the big toe meets the first metatarsal. There is almost a fusion of the joints, which results in an inability to move the big toe. Since the big toe is vital to walking—it is the last area to leave the ground as you push off with each step—hallux limitus can be a debilitating condition.

Several methods are now available to alleviate this condition. These include orthotic devices, custom-fitted shoes, and surgery, in which the joint is actually removed and the base of the big toe realigned and almost reconstructed or an artificial joint implanted.

Heel Pain

Many walkers are all too familiar with heel pain. The most common cause of heel discomfort is a condition called plantar fasciitis. This is an inflammation that occurs at the point where ligaments and muscles in the sole of the foot attach to the heel bone. The telltale sign is pain in the heel, radiating into the middle of the sole, when you first put your foot on the floor in the morning. As you walk around during the day, the pain usually diminishes somewhat, but your foot still will not feel as good as it should.

People with high arches or flat feet are prone to develop plantar fasciitis. Also, pronation (when the heel of the foot rolls either inward or outward with each step) contributes to the problem. Make sure your shoes have good support around the heels and arches. Ice and taping the foot should help ease the pain of plantar fasciitis.

Other causes of heel pain are bone bruises and bony growths on the heel bone, which generally are a result of walking on hard surfaces, stepping on sharp objects, or wearing uncushioned shoes. These growths can be confirmed with an X ray and are often the result of the loss of heel padding due to age. Improper stretching may also cause heel pain. Stretching the Achilles tendon well before walking may help prevent it. (See chapter 4 for stretching exercises.)

Commercial heel pads and heel cups are recommended for preventing heel pain because they take some pressure off the heel. Those with heel pain should wear very flat shoes with a good arch. If you have heel pain when you walk, put ice on the area after exercising.

Aspirin or other anti-inflammatory medicine will keep inflammation down and is especially helpful during the twenty-four hours immediately after pain and swelling appear. But such relief is temporary—equivalent to taking aspirin for relieving a toothache. Generally, orthotic devices specially molded to your feet, arch supports, or proper shoes can alleviate heel pain on a permanent basis.

Weak Arches

Lengthening of the ligaments that run along the arch of the foot causes weak arches. The condition is hereditary, but it can also be caused by overweight and from being on the feet a lot. It is difficult to strengthen weak arches, though such exercises as toe curling, toe stretching, and foot rotation are often used in an attempt. Once arches are weak or collapsed, support may be needed from proper shoes or othotics (see chapter 10). It is best to consult a foot specialist for the best method for dealing with this problem.

Strains and Sprains

Strain and *sprain* are often used interchangeably, but they are not the same. A strain is a stretch or tear in a muscle or tendon, the latter of which connects muscle to bone. A sprain is a stretch or tear of a ligament, which connects bones at a joint.

Strains can occur when you exercise without warming up sufficiently, when muscles are exposed to very cold weather, or when a great deal of stress is placed on a muscle. Any muscle can be strained, but the most susceptible are the hamstrings, at the back of your thighs, and the quadriceps, at the front of the thighs. If you get a strain, put ice on the area as soon as possible, and continue applying ice periodically for forty-eight hours to keep the swelling down. Rest is also advised.

Sprains most commonly occur in the ligaments of the knee or ankle or in the connective tissue of the arch. You can get a sprain by twisting your ankle in a pothole or by stepping off the curb the wrong way.

Perhaps the most succinct advice offered on the treatment of sprains comes from Dr. Robert Nirschl, medical

director of the Virginia Sports Medicine Institute and orthopedic consultant to the President's Council on Physical
Fitness. He suggests all sprain victims remember the
acronym PRICE.

* **P**rotect and immobilize the injured area. If you have
twisted your ankle, keep your shoe on until you are able to
put ice on the injury.

* **R**est. Do not walk or apply unnecessary pressure to
the injured area if you can help it.

* **I**ce. Application of ice reduces swelling and pain and
facilitates healing. Put ice in a towel or plastic bag. Dr.
Nirschl recommends holding the ice on the injured area for
thirty minutes, removing for thirty, then repeating. Do not
apply ice for too long, or frostbite can set in.

* **C**ompress the injury by applying an elastic bandage
to limit swelling. Do not wrap the bandage too tight; you do
not want to cut off blood circulation.

* **E**levate. Keep the sprained area higher than your
heart. This is important for reducing swelling and inflammation. Since elevation serves the same purpose as compres-
sion, you can stop compressing the injury once you are able
to elevate it.

Shinsplints

Shinsplints is a colloquial term for tendonitis involving the
tibial muscles. The pain of shinsplints is felt along the front
of the tibia, or shinbone. Two muscles are involved—the
posterior muscle, whose primary function is to control lock-
ing of the foot; and the anterior muscle, whose primary
function is to act as a shock absorber for the leg below the
knee and whose secondary function is to help lock the foot
in position.

Shinsplints can be caused by walking on concrete or
other hard surfaces, by excessive flexing of the foot, or by
structural problems of the legs. To help prevent shinsplints,
be sure your shoes fit properly and offer enough padding

and support for your feet. Make sure the heels on your shoes are not worn, and avoid walking on hard surfaces if at all possible.

The cure for shinsplints depends on the cause. There is no one major cause, nor is there one major solution. Exercises may help strengthen weak muscles, and orthotic supports of some kind may help correct structural problems. Some persons may have complex problems and may need a combination of exercises and orthotic supports for successful treatment. It is best to consult your podiatrist or orthopedist for specific advice, since incorrect treatment for the condition can make the problem worse.

Achilles Tendonitis

An inflammation of the Achilles tendon is easily identifiable by pain and stiffness between the calf muscle and the heel about an hour after exercising. There may also be a slight swelling. Your walking shoes could be to blame for this problem. A shoe heel that is too low or a shoe counter that is not balanced correctly for your foot may be the cause. Icing the area and taking a rest from your walking program until the pain subsides will help, as will getting good shoes.

It is important to treat this condition properly, since it may indicate the first stage in disease of the tendon.

Knee Injuries

Knees, like ankles, may suffer sprains, and, in this case, the PRICE prescription holds. Often knee problems don't respond particularly well to rest because they are chronic and due to some biomechanical aberration in gait. One cause of knee problems for walkers is putting more of their weight, often unconsciously, on one knee.

Like many other injuries, knee problems are often caused by excessive pronation. When the foot rolls to one side, extra strain is put on the knee joint. In this case, good heel support or orthotics may help.

It is important to consult a physician if you have frequent or chronic knee pain.

Leg or Foot Cramps

Cramps commonly appear in legs and feet and may be caused by dehydration, fatigue, cold, an imbalance of salt or potassium (an important electrolyte used to maintain proper muscle activity and fluid levels), being in the same position for a long period, a muscle imbalance, or even a sharp blow to the foot. To relieve the pain, stretch and knead the cramping area; then apply heat and continue massaging the foot. Cramps often arise mysteriously—and often subside just as mysteriously—but a few precautions may reduce the chances of cramping. Be sure to warm up well before exercising, stop exercising before fatigue sets in, and eat a balanced diet. In addition, drink plenty of water before, during, and after exercising.

Muscle Soreness

Almost everyone who exercises has had sore muscles at one time or another. If you use muscles that haven't been called on in a while, overwork those you have been using, change your exercise routine suddenly, or don't warm up or cool down properly, the result can be sore muscles. Usually the soreness isn't apparent immediately, but shows up within twenty-four hours after you exercise. With no warning sign, it is difficult to know when you are doing something wrong until it is too late.

Doctors once believed that sore muscles were caused by metabolic waste products cast off by muscles during exercise; however, this theory has not been proved. "The most plausible explanation," says Dr. Bryant Stamford in an article in *The Physician and Sportsmedicine,* "is a tissue damage theory. Considerable evidence supports the idea that exercise damages muscle fibers and/or surrounding connective tissue. The muscle tissue becomes swollen, which stimulates sensitive nerve endings and results in soreness."

Muscle soreness usually disappears within a few days. Massage and heat may temporarily relieve the ache, and it often helps to continue exercising during the recovery period, but at a less intense level. If the pain is severe, do not try to work through it; rest is probably the best approach.

To prevent muscle soreness, remember to proceed gradually, and always warm up and cool down properly. When you stretch, do not bounce—stretch out slowly and gently.

Side Stitches

A sudden sharp pain in the side may be the result of improper breathing or a spasm of the diaphragm, which may be put under stress by too-vigorous walking. Often the pain will go away if you slow down a bit. If not, work through the stitch by bending forward and breathing deeply, pushing your stomach out. If that does not work, you can relieve some of the pain by holding your side, lying on your back—if you can find a park bench or other flat surface—and raising your feet in the air. This will help relieve pressure on the diaphragm muscle and restore proper blood circulation to that area.

Chest Pains

Acute pain in the chest area can cause a great deal of anxiety. Any pain or tightness in the chest could be angina pectoris, which occurs when one or more of the coronary arteries has narrowed because of the buildup of fatty deposits. Thus, the heart does not get enough oxygen. Many times angina is the first sign of heart disease.

Angina pectoris is felt as a heaviness or tightness in the chest area, and sometimes there is a burning sensation. The pain sometimes radiates to the arms, shoulders, jaw, or head. Most often angina pectoris is brought on by excitement or fairly strenuous exercise, such as a brisk walk, and lasts no more than five minutes. The symptoms usually go away with rest.

Pain in the chest, however, could also be caused by a pulled muscle in the chest area or on the side of the body. In this case, the area will be tender to the touch, and you will probably feel the pain even after you stop exercising. With time, the discomfort should go away as the muscle heals. Chest pains may also be caused by heartburn. A simple, blander diet may help alleviate the problem.

To distinguish angina pectoris from other chest pains, watch for a feeling of pressure on your chest during exercise or a dull pain that radiates to other parts of your body. If you feel such pain, do not take any risks. Stop exercising, and see your doctor immediately. By the time you feel the symptoms of angina, an artery or arteries have probably narrowed by 60 percent or more.

Suggestions for Relieving Pain

If you experience discomfort while walking, here are a few other bits of advice to help make your walking what it should and can be—painless and pleasure-filled.

Foot massages are excellent for stimulating circulation or helping injuries heal. You can do this by yourself or have someone do it for you. Use lotion, and massage gently, toward your heart. Start with the toes and massage upward; you want to increase blood flow in the direction of the heart because gravity causes blood to pool at the feet. The older you get, the more beneficial massage is. You can also massage feet with an empty soda bottle or a vibrating foot massager.

Body massages, too, are an excellent, and very enjoyable, way to relieve those little aches. Trade massages with a spouse or a friend—why not with a walking buddy? Start by rubbing the neck and shoulder area, which is where a lot of tension accumulates. Then gently massage the hands and work up the arms. Next, rub up the legs toward the trunk of the body; again, this helps circulation. Then move to the back; when you massage this area, be sure not to put pressure on the spine. Spend a little more time kneading areas that your partner says are particularly sore. Or, you can massage your own aching muscles to help them heal.

Whirlpool baths—or hot tubs or Jacuzzis, as they are also called—provide a combination of heat and light massaging action, thanks to the swirling water in the baths. The gentle massage and heat are wonderfully soothing for sore joints and muscles and can help speed healing. Whirlpools are especially good for older people for enhancing circulation. There are a few warnings concerning hot tubs, however: Do not stay in one longer than about five minutes, and never drink alcohol while in the tub or get into one if you have been drinking. Check with your doctor before using a hot tub, since the combination of some medications and heat can cause problems.

Contrast baths are also effective circulation stimulators. Alternate warm and cool soaks for the feet. Soak your feet in warm water (98° F to 102° F) for four minutes; then soak them in cool water (65° F to 75° F) for one minute. Repeat the process four times, ending with a cool soak.

Even if walking causes extreme pain because of arthritis or some other debilitating disease or injury, you may not have to give up walking as exercise. Several hospitals and universities around the country have walking pools, in which people who feel too much pain walking on dry land can do their "laps." At Duke University Medical Center, the entire walking pool is three and a half feet deep and about twenty-five yards long. "The main problem with elderly people is that they have a high risk of orthopedic problems, so you want to minimize the stress to their bones," says Dr. James A. Blumenthal, from the Duke University Preventive Approach to Cardiology program. "The buoyancy of the water takes a lot of the stress off of the joints, and the participants get resistance from the water, so their heart rate rises."

Don't let all this talk of injuries and aches scare you. Walking is still one of the safest ways to work out. With common sense and the knowledge of how to prevent and treat injuries, you can make sure that it stays that way for you.

(10)

Shoes

Nothing can help prevent those little aches that sometimes come from walking as well as a good pair of shoes. Since your feet hit the ground between 1,800 and 2,000 times over the course of a mile, the shoes you choose can make the difference between comfort and pain, between walking as a health benefit and walking as a health hazard. So take the time and effort to choose the right pair, and your feet will repay you for miles to come. Since good walking shoes generally cost between thirty-five dollars and a hundred dollars, it is worth the trouble to find the right ones.

Podiatrists estimate that 80 percent of all adults have complaints about their feet and that half of these problems could be prevented by wearing a certain pair of shoes. If you have ever walked any distance in the wrong shoes, you learned the hard way that bad shoes equal pain. It is not only the feet that take a beating, but the whole body. Proper shoes allow your whole body to function at its best, with minimum discomfort and maximum enjoyment.

These days, it is common to see women wearing sneakers with their suits and dresses on their way to work (men, too, have been spotted in sneakers with their suits). In these health-conscious times, comfort has finally won out over fashion. In response to the demand, many shoe manufacturers are coming out with walking-shoe styles that combine fashion and function so that you no longer have to choose between good looks and comfort.

One such manufacturer is the Rockport Company, which claims to have pioneered the concept of marrying running-shoe comfort with street-shoe style and has received the American Podiatric Medical Association seal of approval for foot therapeutics. The idea seems to be paying off. In 1985, the company's sales rose 45 percent. Many of the leading running-shoe companies are recognizing the need for good walking shoes and are coming out with their own models. Nike, Converse, New Balance, and Brooks, for example, have introduced or are planning to introduce walking shoes. Now that there are many comfortable shoes on the market, the problem is choosing between the different styles.

Finding the Right Shoe

Many walkers have worn running shoes without any problems, and you, too, may find that you prefer running shoes. There are some important difference, however, between running and walking shoes. The most obvious is the look. Walking shoes look more like regular street shoes. In addition, an essential feature of a good walking shoe that a running shoe may not have is a sole that is curved from the heel to the toe. (This, of course, is only good if your forefoot curves similarly.) This allows a smooth, natural shift of weight from the heel to the toe. Your foot doesn't have to flex as much at the ball joint; the result is less fatigue over long distances. Also, most running shoes have treads that help the shoe grip the ground every time it lands. Often the foot continues to slide forward in the shoe with each step. This can cause redness, soreness, and blisters. Walking shoes generally do not have such a heavy tread, and thus your foot is less likely to move forward with each step.

You should look for shoes that lace up rather than slip on. If you walk in slip-ons, your toes will have to grab the bottom of the shoe; after an extended amount of time, this

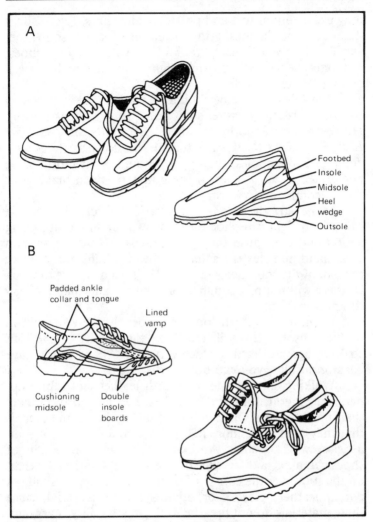

Lightweight walking shoes are specifically designed to give you support under the arches. In A, the thickness of the outsole varies depending on shoe size, providing greater support for those who need it. The shoes shown in B are constructed with a combined last that prevents the foot from slipping inside the shoe as you walk.

may cause discomfort and possibly shinsplints. Laced shoes do not rely on the toes' grip to keep the shoes on, so the toes can flex freely with each step. When you lace your shoes, pull only the top two crossings tight, since feet tend to swell as they exercise.

The sole of the shoe should be made of crepe (crinkled rubber) or rubber; leather soles don't absorb shock as well. However, Dr. Timothy P. Shea, the author of *The Over Easy Foot Care Book,* says that if you do wear shoes with crepe or rubber soles, the uppers should be of fabric or be perforated because soles of these materials can make your feet uncomfortably warm.

Make sure the sole isn't too stiff or thick. With a sole that is too rigid, the shoe resists your foot's natural flexing action and can cause fatigue and aches. Hold the shoe in your hand and flex the sole. The bend should occur where the ball of the foot meets the shoe. If it bends where the arch is, there will not be enough arch support, and that can lead to knee problems.

For more comfort, look for shoes that have a built-in cushion insole. This will minimize the impact of the foot striking against hard surfaces. If your shoes don't have cushion insoles, you can buy an insert.

Walking shoes come with both leather and fabric uppers. In general, leather is your best bet; it holds up longer than most fabrics. One benefit of fabric shoes, however, is that they tend to be more lightweight, and you do not want a heavy walking shoe. An extra four ounces in a pair of shoes can make a difference of one ton of additional weight on the foot over the course of a mile. Avoid uppers made of patent leather, plastic, or other synthetic material, since these materials do not breathe well. Breathability is very important. The average healthy adult loses half a pint of perspiration through the feet each day.

Whether you are looking at leather or fabric shoes, examine the seams carefully. Any rough inner seams can cause chafing and blisters after a short distance.

The heel height should range from three-eighths to five-eighths of an inch higher than the ball of your foot to give you an added boost forward with each step. A good walking shoe should provide sufficient support at the heel to control the angle at which the foot hits the ground. Squeeze the heel counter of the shoe. If it collapses easily, it will not be firm enough to keep your heel in place, which can lead to ankle, leg, and knee problems.

Proper heel support can help prevent one of the most common problems among walkers—excessive pronation. This occurs when your heel rolls too far outward or inward with each step. In some cases, pronation can lead to knee problems. Better walking shoes curb this tendency by providing reinforcement around the heel and up into the front of the shoe. Some cheaper models use cardboard supports, which will eventually break down. Avoid these. You can buy running shoes that have built-in antipronation features that restrict lateral movement of the heel. Many doctors prescribe orthotic devices—shoe inserts specially cast to the shape of your foot—for excessive pronations.

Proper Fit

Shopping for walking shoes requires more care than shopping for regular street shoes. Any flaws in the fit of walking shoes will be magnified and can throw your whole walking program off. For this reason, take more time with your purchase than you would for other shoes.

Make sure to have both feet measured properly with a standard shoe device, even if you think you know your size. If one foot is larger than the other, which is common, buy the shoes for the larger foot; use padding to make the other shoe fit better. Try on all shoes. Even if you are measured as a size eight, a size-eight shoe in a particular brand may be too small, since shoe sizes are not uniform. Walk around the store for a few minutes. The shoes should feel as good when you are walking in them as they do when you are wearing them sitting down. If they are not comfortable in the store, they are not going to be comfortable out on your walking route. (Don't believe salespeople who say that the shoes will feel better after they have been broken in.) Shop late in the day, when your feet will be at their largest.

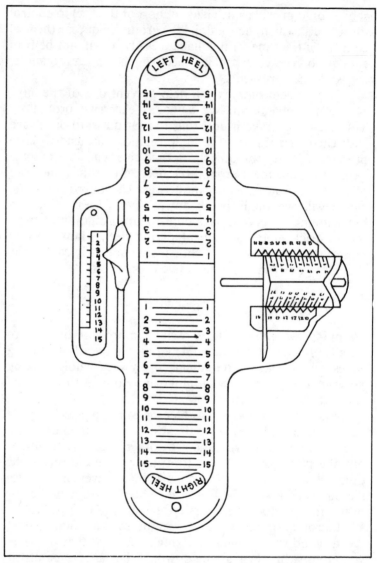

Be sure to have both feet measured for the proper size when you buy walking shoes. This device and ones similar to it measure both the length and width of the foot.

A shoe that fits well must be long enough from the heel of the foot to the ball of the foot so that the shoe breaks in the right place. It must be wide enough to accommodate the ball of the foot. A shoe that fits well also holds your heel snugly to prevent blistering and rubbing. Check the toe box, the front part of the shoe, as well. When you are standing in the shoes, the end of your longest toe (not necessarily your big toe) should be a thumb-width away from the end of the shoe. The toe box should also be wide enough to allow you to wiggle your toes freely. Make sure, too, that the toe box is firm. If it is flimsy, it can easily break down with wear.

After buying a pair of shoes, walk around in them for a few days in your home. Be sure to walk on carpet so that there are no marks on the soles. If your shoes hurt your feet, return them and look for another pair. If they feel good, you can take them out on your walk.

How will you know whether your shoes are doing the job they should? Any pain in the lower legs, knees, arches, or heels or the buildup of calluses after walking are warning signs that your shoes may not be right for you. A podiatrist can point out the specific changes you may need to make in your selection of shoes to wear. (See Appendix B for a listing of companies that manufacture walking shoes and their addresses.)

Caring for Your Shoes

It is a good idea to give your shoes an airing once a week or so. Take out the laces, and lay your shoes in a dry area where air can circulate in and around them. Sunlight will kill the bacteria inside the shoes, but you should not leave your shoes in the sun for more than an hour or two at a time, since excessive exposure can dry out leather uppers and can begin to break down certain synthetic materials.

If you get caught in a downpour and your shoes get sopping wet, stuff the shoes with newspaper, and dry them *away* from any direct heat. They will retain their original shape and flexibility best when dried at room temperature. Always waterproof leather shoes immediately after purchasing them to prevent them from getting ruined in the rain.

Mink oil is particularly good for this. Some silicone water-proofing treatments contain strong chemicals that can break down the glue that holds the layers of the soles together in certain shoes. Ask a shoe salesperson about silicone treatments before applying them to your shoes. There is probably no need to waterproof nylon running shoes, since they dry out very quickly and usually are not damaged by wetness. You may, however, want to waterproof the leather sections on running shoes that are made from a combination of leather and nylon.

Socks

The more absorbent the better, and socks with a high percentage of cotton are generally the most absorbent. Wool is also a good choice, particularly for cooler days. Socks should not be so thick that they constrict the natural movement of the foot inside the shoe. Besides comfort, an important reason for wearing absorbent socks is that they can extend the life of your shoes greatly. The salts and acids in perspiration that are not absorbed by your socks can eat up the insoles of your shoes after a lot of wear, making the shoes uncomfortable. Sweat also can cause rashes and itchiness of your feet if not absorbed into the sock, and heat combined with sweat and pressure from ill-fitting shoes can cause corns. If you walk short distances and your feet do not perspire a great deal, stay away from socks made of synthetic fibers such as nylon because they make the feet sweat more and promote the growth of fungi.

For proper fit, according to the Footwear Council, wear socks that are one-quarter of an inch longer to one-half inch longer than your feet. That means wearing no tube or one-size-fits-all socks; they often fit too tight. Tight socks restrict your toes and cause friction against the whole foot.

Never wear a pair of socks for more than one day without having them washed. If you do, you run the risk of fungal infections. If your socks develop holes, throw them away. Mended areas can irritate the skin.

Orthotics

Orthotic devices are shoe inserts that are specially cast to the shape of your foot—based on a mold of your foot—and made to fit inside a standard shoe. They are prescribed by orthopedists and podiatrists and are designed to improve the stability of the feet. They can be made of sturdy plastic, leather, cork, or rubber. The type of materials used depends on your activities, foot problems, and age. A molded leather and cork device is an excellent shock absorber and most practical for the aging foot. Generally, orthotics cost an average of $150 a pair, though cork ones are usually less expensive. There are also devices for localized pain, such as

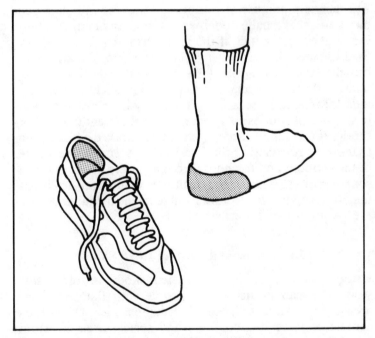

Molded plastic heel cups are a relatively inexpensive way to help cushion the heel. The heel fits snugly into the heel cup, which is inserted into the shoe.

plastic heel cups, that help stabilize the foot and cushion the heel. Generally, these sell for less than twenty dollars. Over-the-counter, mass-produced shoe inserts are inexpensive, but they do not correct specific problems of feet. They are actually only useful for cushioning tired feet.

Orthotics were once believed beneficial for a wide variety of biomechanical problems—from flat feet to knee problems. There has been some recent debate on whether orthotics actually help. Some doctors believe they may cause other problems in wearers that might be worse than the original ailments the devices were supposed to help. In any event, few doctors consider orthotics the cure-all they once thought them to be.

The major reason for prescribing orthotics is to place a specific joint in a neutral position and to limit pronation. Another common use of orthotics in walkers and older people is to relieve pain underneath the metatarsal, the bone that makes up the ball of the foot. Orthotics frequently are used to treat high arches; for this condition, the arches are heavily padded. Scientific tests show that orthotics properly made and fitted are an effective method to help foot and leg muscles function. Because of this, they have become an integral part of foot care. There are now different types of orthotics for different foot structures. Orthotic devices are not that costly considering the fact that they enable the wearer to move about and to choose from a variety of shoes at reasonable prices. Also, more insurance companies are beginning to recognize orthotics as viable medical equipment and are paying for such devices.

Orthopedic and Custom-fitted Shoes

Orthopedic, or specially constructed, shoes are sold in shoe stores and can be helpful to people with flat feet, weak arches, pronation, bunions, and hammertoes. Often these shoes have extended counters and special heels. Custom-fitted shoes are advisable if foot problems cause debilitation or deformity or if feet are sensitive to even slight pressure due to severe diabetes, circulatory problems, or arthritis. While these shoes help many people walk who would not be able to otherwise, they are very expensive. For custom-fitted shoes, a podiatrist or shoemaker must make a plaster mold of each foot. After a first pair has been made, additional pairs are less expensive because the molds of the feet are reusable.

(11)

Optional Gear and Equipment

Simplicity. It is what walking is all about. No fancy steps or swings or moves to learn. No special rackets or outfits or balls to buy. No special places to get to. Just a good pair of shoes and you're off.

You could get along beautifully without investing in anything else except good shoes. Convenience is one reason that walking is so popular. Another reason is that it is so inexpensive.

There are, however, products that, even though not essential, can make your walking safer, more enjoyable, or more beneficial. These range from reflective clothing to personal stereos to heart monitors.

Safety Products

Of all the optional gear and equipment available for purchase, safety products are the most sensible and valuable. They help ensure your safety while you are out on your walking course.

Reflective Gear

If you walk in the early morning hours, in the evening, in fog, or under any conditions where poor visibility may jeopardize your safety, invest in some sort of reflective gear. (Reflective gear is especially useful in the winter, when it gets dark earlier.) You can choose from items you wear over or with your clothes, such as reflective hats, vests, headbands, belts, and ankle straps, which go around the bottoms of your pant legs. Or you can buy reflective tape or patches that you can stick, pin, or sew onto your walking clothes. Or you may want to spend more money to get a reflective nylon exercise suit that will not only allow you to be seen, but also will protect you from rain and wind.

Reflective gear works this way: Specially treated strips, usually in reflective colors or metallic silver, are sewn onto

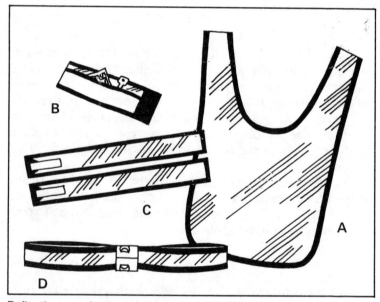

Reflective gear is essential to your safety if you walk under conditions of poor or questionable visibility. A one-size-fits-all vest (A) can be worn over your regular clothing, as can bands (C) and a belt (D). Some of the gear, such as the wrist wallet shown (B), combines safety with practicality.

the products—or, in the case of the reflective tape, the product itself is specially treated. When beams from car headlights, streetlights, or flashlights hit the treated area, they are reflected and shine back very brightly in the dark. Some products are treated with substances that can be seen up to half a mile away.

Make sure that you have reflective strips or patches on your front and on your back so that cars coming in either direction will be able to see you. Wear reflective items around your feet or another moving part so drivers can pick you out more easily and distinguish you from a stationary object, such as a reflective sign on the side of the road.

Reflective jogging suits are a pants and jacket combination, usually made of nylon, polypropylene, or a material called Gore-Tex. They have reflective strips sewn onto various portions of the outfit. If you buy a suit, look for one with reflective strips across the chest, around the sleeves, and around the lower portion of the pants—the more visible you are on the road, the better. Jogging suits are very expensive compared to other reflective products. To get your money's worth, you must wear the jogging suit every time you walk in the dark, which is impractical in the spring and summer.

Lights

Instead of reflective gear, or as an added safety measure, you may want to carry a light to make sure you are seen. You can get a round, blinking light that clips on to your clothes, blinks eighty times per minute, and can be seen up to a mile away. There are also battery-operated lighted wands that are about a foot long; you simply carry one in your hand. Since these devices give off light rather than reflect it, you do not have to be in the beam of a headlight to be seen. This is an advantage if, for example, you walk at night in an unlit park where there may be other walkers passing in either direction.

Sound Alarms

To scare off dogs or attackers, as well as to call for help in an emergency, you may want to carry a sound-emitting device. There is, of course, the old, reliable (and inexpensive) whistle. Put one on a string, and hang it around your neck when you go for a walk. Also on the market are slim aerosol cans that emit shrill, frightening sounds. You can carry one of these easily in your hand or pocket.

Personal Identification Cards

Too often walkers leave their homes without any identification. Because they are only going around the neighborhood or the park, they may not see a need to bring their wallets along. And since most people keep their identification in their wallets, these walkers go out into the world as anonymous souls.

No one likes to think of such things, but what if you had a medical emergency or were attacked by someone and were not conscious to identify yourself? You would definitely want doctors to give you the right medication. You would want the police to call the right people. This is why it is so important to carry an ID card with you at all times when you walk.

You may be able to get a medical ID card from your physician, or you can buy one. As an alternative, you can make your own by including the following on a credit card–sized piece of sturdy paper or poster board: your name, address, and phone number; the name and phone number of a close family member or friend; your physician's name and phone number; your blood type; any medications you are currently using; any allergies you are aware of; and any medical conditions you have. To waterproof the card, remove one of the plastic photo holders from your wallet, and put the card in it. Seal the photo holder with tape.

Put your card in some item you usually have with you when you walk, such as a backpack or a favorite jacket. If you do not wear a specific item during each walk, you may want to leave the ID near your door so that you will remember to bring it along on your way out.

Money

It is always a good idea to carry at least a quarter with you for an emergency phone call.

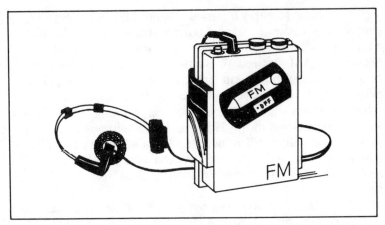

Personal stereos come in assorted sizes and shapes. Many models combine the features of a radio and a cassette player. The model shown here can be clipped to a belt.

Personal Stereos

Personal stereos were introduced in the United States several years ago, and walking hasn't been the same since— it's been better. These stereos can make walking more entertaining and enlightening, and they are more affordable than they have ever been, with some models costing less than twenty dollars. You can listen to your own choice of music through small headphones so that you do not disturb anyone around you. In addition, the stereos are light and will fit into a pocket or clip on to your clothing so that you can walk unencumbered.

You can buy personal stereos with the following features: AM/FM radio, FM radio only, AM radio only, AM/FM radio with cassette player, or cassette player only. Some are the size of a paperback; others are much smaller. Some small models strap around your upper arm, and one model is so compact that the radio receiver is built into the headset. Small nylon packs are specifically made to carry a personal stereo around your waist.

The more features a personal stereo has, the more expensive it will be. If your favorite station is on the AM band, you will save some money by getting a stereo that only broadcasts AM stations. Cassette players are more expensive than radio models, but they have some advantages. You can play the music of your choice—or listen to language instruction tapes—and you will not get the static that you sometimes get on a radio. However, if you do buy a cassette player, you will possibly need to bring along extra tapes, which can become burdensome, and you usually have to replace the batteries more frequently than you do with a radio.

A word of caution: Do not play your personal stereos too loud. Not only does this drown out outside noises, in which case you may not hear an approaching car, but it also can hurt your eardrums. Keep the volume at a moderately soft level.

Packs and Pockets

It is a warm summer day. You are wearing a pair of shorts and a T-shirt. You are planning to walk down to the park and read by the duck pond, but you don't want to hold on to your book for two miles.

You would like to do some errands when you take your walk through town, but you do not want to carry a grocery bag all the way home.

If you ever find yourself in either of the above situations, you'll be glad that you have a pack. Here are some other times when packs are particularly useful: when you want to bring along a picnic lunch, when you want to take a jacket in case the weather turns bad while you are walking, on hot days when you want to carry some extra water, and when you walk home from work and need a place to put your street shoes and your papers. Some people carry a pack every time they walk so they can take along essentials, such as keys and a wallet. Also, if you ever go on a day hike, you will need a backpack (see chapter 14).

The advantage of carrying a pack is that it frees your hands and distributes the weight of your load evenly. Carry-

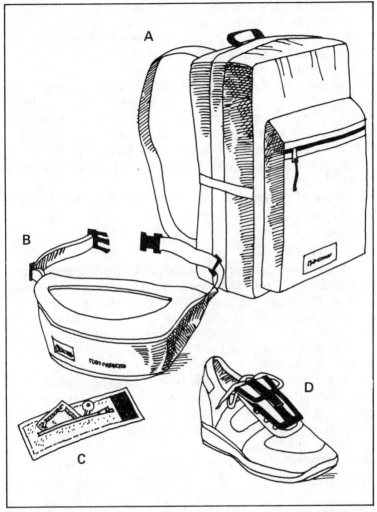

There are packs and pockets for all occasions. The daypack (A) is ideal for light hiking; the outside pockets can be used for notepads, binoculars, or anything else you might want to reach for again and again. The fanny pack (B) leaves your hands free and still allows you to take along a camera or lunch. The flat wrist wallet (C) and shoe pocket (D) are convenient for carrying keys or cash.

ing a ten-pound bag of groceries in your arms for any distance can have an adverse effect on your posture and may strain a muscle or two. Besides, it is quite difficult to do. But the same weight in a pack on your back is much easier to handle—and much easier on your body.

If you have deep pockets in your walking clothes, you could probably do without a pack in many instances. But again, the weight isn't going to be distributed evenly, and it is quite cumbersome to walk at the proper speed with big, bulging pockets. In the summer, when you walk without a jacket, you probably won't have as many pockets in which to put things.

Some of the types of packs now on the market are described below.

Backpacks

Many small backpacks (or daypacks, as light packs are called) are available that are relatively inexpensive—less than twenty dollars. A good quality backpack will be made of heavy, waterproof cordura or oxford nylon material and will have padded, adjustable shoulder straps and an adjustable strap that fits around the waist to keep the pack securely in place.

If you would rather not look as if you are going out to trek along the Appalachian Trail, there are expandable packs that you can wear on your back while walking and then convert to a shoulder bag or briefcase when you want a less sporty appearance.

Backpacks are an ideal place to put reflective tape, and some come with reflective strips on them.

Fanny Packs

These products are small pouches that strap around the waist. They can't hold a great deal, but there is enough room in most of them to carry such items as a camera, a book, lunch, or a flask of water—with space left over. Some come with a flask built into the pack; others are specially designed to carry personal stereos. A good fanny pack will have a padded hip band.

Pockets

If you want something very small in which to carry a few keys and a few dollars, there are a couple of products to choose from. One is a flat "wrist wallet," which is, depending on the manufacturer, about two and a half inches wide and about ten inches long. Running the length of the product is a zippered pocket, in which you can store items. You wrap the wallet around your wrist and secure it with a Velcro closing. It is so light that you quickly forget you are wearing it.

Another useful product is a small rectangular pocket that you can attach to the laces of your shoes or to your belt with a Velcro fastener.

Timing and Measuring Devices

This is where high tech steps into the exercise boom. You can get everything from a talking computer that monitors your heart rate and calculates the number of calories you are burning to a pair of computerized shoes that keep track of your mileage. Obviously, these items are extravagant, but following is a brief guide to some of the more practical timing and measuring devices.

Watches

A good sports watch is not essential, but it is very helpful when you are trying to stick to a walking program. What makes a sports watch good? Well, one thing for sure, it has little to do with the number of features on a particular watch. If you wanted to, you could get watches that give you the outside temperature, tell you the direction in which you are traveling, or store messages to yourself for future recall. One company advertises that its sports watch "does everything but wash your socks."

Ignore all the fancy gizmos, for which you pay dearly, and stick to a watch that provides you with the solid basics. These include time in hours, minutes, and seconds; the date; and the ability to record elapsed time like a stopwatch so that you will be able to get a precise reading of the amount of time your walk took. The stopwatch feature can be used

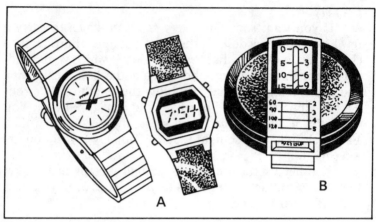

Good sports watches (A) are helpful to all walking programs. A pedometer (B) shows you the distance you have walked and the number of steps you have taken.

to count off ten seconds when measuring your heart rate. (A timepiece that incorporates a stopwatch is called a chronograph.) Also, you will probably want what is called a "time in/time out" feature. This allows you to stop the timer if you pause during your walk and then start it again when you resume walking. This is particularly convenient if you stop along your way to talk to a friend or for a stoplight. You should be able to get a watch with these features for less than thirty dollars.

Here is what to look for when you are shopping for a watch: The lens should be of glass rather than plastic, which is easy to scratch and may become difficult to see through. The watch case should be lightweight and made of durable materials. Most sports watches have a black plastic band; make sure it is lightweight yet strong. Polyurethane is the best material for the band. Metal bands are certainly durable, but they make the watch heavier, and some people find them cumbersome and uncomfortable.

It is a good idea to get a sports watch that is waterproof (most of them are), since you will be sweating while wearing it and may be walking in the rain with it on. Look for a high-contrast digital display for easy reading and a back light, which you can use if you are walking in the dark. The stopwatch and other functions should be easy to set.

Heart Rate Monitors

You will find several pulse monitors on the market. One model is small enough to slip over one of your fingers. Throughout your walk, a microchip monitors your heart rate, which is registered on a digital display. There is a larger model that you hold in your hand while you walk, keeping your thumb on a metal sensor. After every eight heartbeats, your heart rate is calculated and displayed. The numbers these devices come up with are not always accurate; the reading on many often depends on how much pressure you put against the sensor with your finger.

Some fitness experts recommend using a monitor that you attach to your chest because it gives a more precise reading. However, such products are relatively expensive. Besides, you can take your heart rate with the most reliable, cheapest device around—your fingers.

Pedometers

Although you will probably be walking for time instead of distance, at some point you may want to know how much mileage you are covering. To do this, you can walk along a premeasured route or on a track, you can measure the distance you have covered on your car's odometer, or you can wear a pedometer. The advantages of a pedometer are that you do not have to stick to a predetermined course, and every step is taken into account (such as if you walk back and forth across a street to check out sale items in store windows). It is also helpful if you walk in a park or an area where you cannot measure the distance by car.

Inside a pedometer is a pendulum that swings each time you take a step and that increases the mileage by the length of each step. (Pedometers have adjustable meters on which you can set your step length.) The cumulative distance is recorded on the dial of the instrument.

One good way to determine the length of your step is to walk a measured distance on soft ground and divide the distance by the number of foot impressions. For example, if you took ten steps to walk twenty-five feet, your step length is two and a half feet. You could also measure from the heel of one footprint to the heel of another.

Most pedometers are not completely accurate—since your step length can vary during a walk, such as when you go up or down a hill—but they are good rough estimates. To get a more precise reading, try to walk at a steady, even pace.

Walking Sticks

For centuries, people have carried walking sticks for a variety of reasons—for balance, for safety, or for fashion. In ancient times, travelers used walking sticks that were bent on one end to fight off bandits as well as to pull down the high branches of fruit trees. Sometime in the seventeenth century, walking sticks became fashionable, and kings, emperors, and presidents are known to have had finely crafted staffs close at hand. In addition, walking sticks have in the past doubled as guns and pipes. One model reportedly converted into a bicycle.

But, fortunately, you can do without the frills if you decide you would like to bring a stick along on your strolls. All you need is a plain old stick from a tree in your yard or neighborhood. This is one piece of equipment that you can obtain absolutely free. Make sure it is sturdy and straight and a height you feel comfortable with. A handy length for a walking stick is the height to your shoulders. (A good, handmade walking stick can be ordered through The Hermann Werks, RR 1 Box 60 A (W), Hermann, Missouri 65041; telephone number, 1-314-486-2747. Choose from rustic sticks of knotted wood or sleek, polished canes with metal tips.)

Some walkers use sticks for balance and for help getting up hills. Others generally use them for rhythm, tapping the ground with each step to keep the pace. Still others use

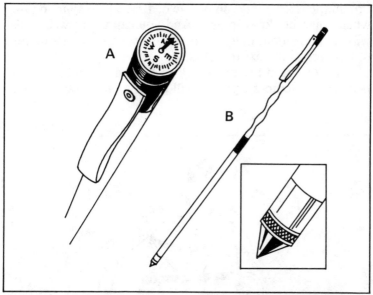

Walking sticks come in many shapes and sizes. Some have added equipment such as a compass in the head (A). Others simply help provide balance and a walking rhythm. A pointed tip (inset, B) is useful if you plan to walk over rough terrain or on hilly trails.

them as a protection from dogs. And almost all become very attached to the chosen staff, never setting out on a walk without it.

Treadmills

Do your walking right in your own home. Walk in perfect weather year-round.

It sounds enticing. That is why many people buy treadmills. That is why you, too, may be tempted to get one. With a treadmill, you never have to worry about rain, cold, snow, or what route you will take. But what you do have to worry about is the monotony. There is no scenery, no variation in the terrain, and no breeze or fresh air to spur you on when you feel like stopping. And you can't very well walk with a companion, unless a friend or your spouse sets up his or her treadmill next to yours.

There is another drawback to treadmills—they are expensive. Sometimes a person will invest up to $2,000 in one,

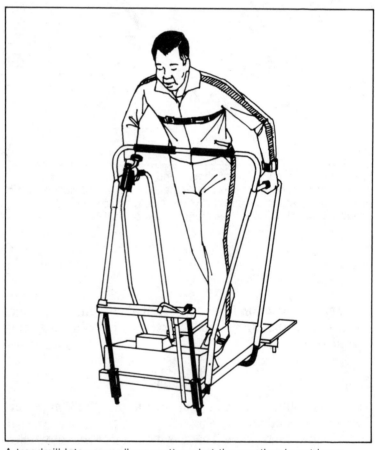

A treadmill lets you walk no matter what the weather is outdoors. The side rails help provide balance as you increase your pace.

thinking it is the answer to his or her exercise dilemma. However, after a few months, monotony squelches the use of it—and sometimes the whole exercise program. Treadmills are either manual or motorized, with manual ones being cheaper. But still, you generally cannot get a good manual one for less than $500, and a good electric treadmill will cost you at least $1,000. You can save your money and walk outside, where it is free as well as scenic. If the weather is a problem, do your walking in a mall or gym. (If, however, you have used a treadmill regularly before, say at an exercise club, and have found it very useful, you may want to consider getting one for your home. But try cheaper forms of exercise before you invest.)

Weights

By carrying weights while you walk, you can burn off additional calories. More weight means your body will have to work harder against the pull of gravity, and that means more energy will be used. For this reason, many people use ankle and/or hand weights during exercise.

Many types of weights are available. You can buy a pair of weights that you attach to your shoes by stringing the laces through holes in the weights; a set comes with eight half-pound weights so that you can gradually increase your strength and endurance. There are also weights that strap around your ankles. One model is a flat, flexible weight wrapped in vinyl-covered foam, and another model is made of a soft, synthetic material covered with padded terry cloth. Neither model allows you to adjust the amount of weight you carry. It is wise to check with your doctor before using any ankle weights, since they have been known to cause shinsplints.

You have a few more options with hand weights. You can carry small, light dumbbells, or you can buy special gloves that have compartments for weights, allowing you to adjust the amount of weight and to exercise without gripping anything. There are weights that you can strap around your wrists that are identical to the models described above for ankles. And there is also the brand of weights called

Heavyhands, which has done much to popularize the practice of walking with weights. Heavyhands have a center bar to hold on to and, on either end, relatively light weights (you can add heavier weights as you progress in your walking program). They look like dumbbells, except that Heavyhands also have a padded metal band that passes over the back of your hand when you hold the center bar.

Dr. Leonard Schwartz, the inventor of Heavyhands, says that most people's legs are more fit than their arms, since the former support and carry around their bodies. Walking with Heavyhands (or any light hand weights) strengthens your arms and the muscles of your upper torso that usually are not worked during regular walking. This increases your calorie expenditure and your overall cardiovascular fitness.

Some doctors remain unconvinced, however. "I've seen little data to support the idea that you'll get great cardiovascular benefits from hand-weight work," Jim Hodgson, associate professor of applied physiology at Penn State University says. In addition, there is concern that hand weights elevate diastolic blood pressure.

Dr. Schwartz maintains that you should have no problems if you progress with a weight-walking program gradually. You can adjust the intensity of your regimen to your fitness level in three ways. Using more weight is one way, and the speed at which you swing your arms is another. Also, the higher you swing your arms, the more difficult the exercise level. Thus, a person who is not very fit should probably start with one-pound weights in each hand, swinging them slowly and not very high.

If you want to try walking with weights, do not begin until you can comfortably walk with your heart rate at your target level for an extended period, for example, forty-five minutes. It's wise to make sure you can pull your own weight easily before taking on any more.

(12)

Rain, Dogs, and Other Special Conditions

Oh, if only all your walks could be taken on pristine days with the temperature in the mid sixties and a slight breeze to pick up your hair and your mood. Then, maybe, sticking to a walking program would be as easy as sticking to a diet of ice-cream sundaes. But one of the facts of walking is that you will not be exercising in ideal conditions every time you go out; you may occasionally have to face such vexations as rain, cold, heat, and dogs. The best thing you can do is be well prepared to handle weather and other environmental conditions so that you do not have to drop your walking plans at the first drop of rain. If you are a fair-weather walker, you may find that you are staying home more than you are walking.

Most likely there will be several days out of the year when you should not exercise outside—in a raging blizzard, for example. But in general, with proper dress and proper safety measures, you will be able to go out on most any day, and you will probably find that you actually enjoy some of the weather conditions that you used to dread. A park blanketed with snow has a serene charm, and a summer rainfall gives the air a wonderfully fresh smell and provides a cool contrast to normal summer heat as well as a rhythmic background sound. Getting out regularly, even in less-than-perfect weather, will make you feel as if you have more control over your environment (since you are not letting it control you), and that adds to your sense of mastery and self-esteem.

There are some precautions, however, that you can and should take to make your walks free from irritation and danger.

Heat

Most people are more active in summer than in any other season. You see people out everywhere from Memorial Day to Labor Day, playing tennis or golf, jogging, and taking walks on beaches or in parks. Many of these exercisers wouldn't think about going out in the cold of January. Ironically, summer's heat causes more health problems than any other environmental condition in which you will be walking, including freezing temperatures.

Your moving body generates heat, and usually your body is able to maintain a temperature of 98.6° F through a sophisticated temperature-regulation system that controls the amount of heat your body retains or loses. This is where perspiration comes in. The evaporation of sweat from the surface of your skin is your body's most effective cooling device. This system works fine and well under most circumstances, but when you get out in high heat and push yourself too hard, overdress, or fail to drink enough liquids, it's a different story. Your body is not able to rid itself of the heat it produces as efficiently when the surrounding temperature is extremely hot. High humidity only makes the problem worse; your sweat will evaporate more slowly, since the air will not be able to hold as much moisture as it can on a dry day.

If you continue to exercise heavily in high heat and humidity, your body temperature will rise, which can lead to the following conditions.

1. Heat cramps in muscles, such as the calves, which usually result from dehydration. They are often the first sign of trouble.

2. Heat exhaustion, which occurs when the brain does not get enough blood because most of the blood is going to blood vessels near the skin to be cooled. This condition can result in headache, confusion, or unconsciousness.

3. Heat stroke, the most serious condition, which occurs when the body's temperature rises to dangerous levels, in some cases reaching 110° F. Symptoms include dizziness, diarrhea, vomiting, and confusion.

It is wise, therefore, to follow these precautions when hoofing in the heat.

1. Drink plenty of water. This is the first and foremost rule of warm-weather exercising. Drink it long before you go out, during your walk (pick a route that takes you by a water fountain), and afterward. Dehydration is a serious condition that is a primary contributor to the three heat-distress syndromes mentioned above. You can lose as much as three quarts of body fluid (six pounds of body weight) in one hour through the evaporation of perspiration. If you don't replace those fluids, the body cannot sweat to cool itself down. Don't wait until you are thirsty to drink, since thirst is not a good indicator of how much fluid you need—you usually need a lot more than the amount it takes to quench your thirst.

Unless you walk great distances and perspire heavily, you should not have any problem with loss of the essential minerals needed to maintain fluid balance in the body and transmit nerve impulses to your muscles.

Putting water directly on your body also seems to help cool it. On a hot day, you may want to splash your face and arms with water at a fountain during your walk. If you have a bandanna or cloth with you, it is helpful to wet it and gently apply it to the large veins on either side of your neck. This will help cool your blood.

2. Go easy, especially on the first hot days of the season. It takes your body seven to ten days to adjust to the hot weather; then you can walk a little faster. After you are accustomed to the heat, you still should not walk as briskly as you do in cooler weather—just to be safe.

3. Dress in loose, lightweight clothing. By exposing as much skin as possible, your body will lose more heat. Wear light-colored shorts and a T-shirt, or better yet, a nylon mesh tank top. Heavy clothes prevent heat from escaping and inhibit the evaporation of sweat. Tight clothes become soaked quickly, cling to the skin, and retard the production of sweat. If you are uncomfortable in shorts, wear light-colored cotton pants. Light-colored clothing reflects the sun; dark colors absorb the heat. You may want to wear a light-colored hat or a visor to protect your face and head from the sun (bald men, especially, should wear a hat).

4. Avoid walking in the middle of the day in warm weather. Try to go out early in the morning or in the evening, when the temperatures are cooler. The worst time to be out in the sun is 11:00 A.M. to 2:00 P.M. Remember the saying "Mad dogs and Englishmen go out in the midday sun." Not only are you more likely to suffer from heat injury, but you are also more likely to get sunburned.

5. Wear sunscreen whenever you walk in the sun, even if it is before 11:00 A.M. or after 2:00 P.M.—you can still get sunburned in nonpeak hours. Too much sun makes your skin age faster, causing premature dryness, sagging, wrinkling, and the development of liver spots. When you buy a sunscreen, look for one with a sun protection factor (SPF) of fifteen, which by current standards is the strongest available. It gives you fifteen times more protection than untreated skin. Alcohol-based sunscreens are better than oil- or cream-based ones because the alcohol quickly evaporates in the sun, leaving only the sunscreen. Greasy sunscreens will clog your pores and won't allow your body to throw off heat as efficiently.

Exposure to sun can have an adverse effect on such medical conditions as diabetes and circulatory problems; it can also aggravate skin conditions such as eczema and certain rashes. In addition, a number of drugs can worsen your reaction to the sun. These include some antibiotics, namely certain tetracyclines; artificial sweeteners; diabetes medications such as Diabinese and Orinase; diuretics, particularly chlorothiazides; and certain antihistamines, such as Phenergan. Ask your doctor if the drugs you take will change your sensitivity to sunlight.

6. Stay away from hot pavement. Black asphalt heats up very quickly, and walking on it will only add to your heat buildup. Try to walk on concrete sidewalks or grass paths instead.

Cold

At the other extreme is walking in the cold, which is probably more dreaded than walking in the heat. Just because the thermometer dips below the forty-degree mark does not mean that all exercising should stop. You are going to have to fight that little voice telling you to stay inside. You can get out much of the winter as long as you take some cold-combating precautions. There are, of course, times you shouldn't go out—in a blizzard, for one, and when the temperature falls well below freezing, when there is danger of frostbite or hypothermia. Check, too, the windchill factor, which makes it feel much colder than the thermometer indicates (see the chart on page 158 to find out how to determine windchill). If it is really nasty out, you can do what John Chin, a fifty-nine-year-old walker, does and head to the nearest mall for your walk. "It's a nice controlled temperature inside. It's very pleasant."

To keep your body at a controlled temperature when you walk outside in winter, you should make getting dressed one of the most important parts of your walk. It is best to wear several layers of thin, breathable clothing rather than single layers of thick, bulky clothing that inhibits your movement. Three layers is probably the most you will need. Layering will allow you to remove clothing as necessary if you get too warm. For example, put on a long-sleeved cotton underwear top or a cotton turtleneck next to your skin; over that, wear a hooded sweatshirt that zips shut. A zippered garment is more versatile than a pullover because you can adjust your temperature by unzipping the garment if necessary. On top of these items, wear an easy-to-open, lightweight nylon jacket to protect yourself against the wind without adding weight. On very cold days, you will probably need a heavier, lined jacket. Your legs don't need to be clothed in as many layers, since they will be doing the most work on your walk and thus generating quite a bit of heat. A pair of sweatpants, and in very cold weather a pair of thermal underwear underneath, should be all you need on your legs.

You might be a little cool when you start off (if you warm up properly, though, you will be less so), but after walking for a time, your body will become warmer as it produces heat. As soon as you begin to perspire, you should unzip your jacket so your sweat can evaporate. You can get cold 200 times faster in sweat-soaked clothing than in dry clothing. You may want to take off your jacket completely if you get excessively warm. Just make sure that after you take off an item, you don't stop moving until you get back inside. If you stop while your jacket is off, your body will cool down fast, and you may become chilled.

On cold days, a hat is extremely important, since much body heat is lost through the head. A cap can conserve as much as 40 percent of your body heat. You may find that the cold air hurts your lungs when you breathe in. If this happens, you may want to cover your mouth and nose with a light scarf and concentrate on breathing through your nose, as this will preheat the air before it enters the lungs. A hood that covers your head and comes up over your mouth will work too. It is advisable to wear a ski mask at temperatures of 0° F and below.

It is a good idea to wear mittens instead of gloves. Mittens keep the fingers together, thus providing more warmth. Woolen liners under a leather shell offer the most protection.

Cold feet are a common complaint in winter. Feet are more sensitive to the cold than are hands because less blood flows to the feet. Your feet will stay warmest in wool socks and a leather shoe with a felt liner, though some synthetics may be even better than leather if it is wet outdoors. Even though you may like to wear lightweight nylon athletic shoes the rest of the year, it is better to wear more substantial leather shoes when it is cold and snowy. Leather shoes will provide greater warmth and will give you more secure footing on ice and snow. If your feet get cold continuously—no matter what you wear—check to make sure you are not tying your laces too tightly, and cutting off circulation. If it is not your laces, you may want to check with your doctor, since cold feet are a symptom of diabetes and of Raynaud's disease, a circulatory disorder. Try to limit your caffeine intake and your cigarette smoking, if you smoke, particularly in the winter, since both make your blood vessels constrict, and your extremities may not get the amount of blood they need to keep warm. Two areas of the body are particularly susceptible to the cold: the nipples and the penis. Be sure that these areas are adequately protected when you walk outside in cold weather.

Falls are a major problem with winter walking. Each year tens of thousands of people are injured from falls, many of these occurring from November through March in the northeastern and mid-Atlantic states, and many victims are elderly. Anticipating icy conditions goes a long way in keeping you off the ground. Slow your pace down, and scan the surface ahead for white frosted areas. If you know where puddles usually form around your home and neighborhood, expect to find ice there in the wintertime. One of the most likely slippery situations is when snow melts during the day and then freezes at night, leaving clear sheets of ice on pavement in the morning.

If you do hit a patch of ice, take short steps while keeping your knees bent slightly and your body weight over the balls of your feet. Hold your arms in front of you at waist level for balance.

A lot of injuries can be avoided if you know how to fall properly. If you feel yourself falling backward, do not put your arms out behind you to break your fall; you could end up breaking an arm or wrist. You should move into the fall by bending your knees and attempting to bring your buttocks as close to your feet as possible. This way, you won't be falling at such a distance. When you hit the ground, relax, and roll backward with the momentum of the fall. If you start to fall forward, do not try to break the fall with your arms. Again, bend your knees, and when you make contact with the ground, do not stop moving. Continue moving into the fall. If you must use your arms to stop yourself from falling on your face, bend them slightly to use as shock absorbers.

One of the most serious mistakes a winter exerciser can make is going outside without warming up properly. Stretching after you exercise is also more important in cold weather in order to work out the tightness brought on by the cold.

Wind

You will notice wind only when it is blowing at about eight to ten miles per hour. When you walk into strong wind, keep your head down, lean into the wind, and pump your arms harder. Wind is usually only a problem in low temperatures. If it is cold and windy out, plan your route so that you travel into the wind on the first half of your route. Because windchill can increase the dangers of cold weather exposure, you should face the most gusty part while you are fresh and dry. You may be uncomfortable for five or ten minutes, but you will warm up quickly. Your return will be easier, with the wind at your back to push you along. Or on a particularly windy day, you may want to have someone drive you to a location that will allow you to do your entire walk with the wind at your back.

The table below, based on information from the National Weather Service, shows how winds of various speeds make it feel colder than the actual temperatures by creating a windchill effect.

Windchill Factor
(Equivalent temperature on exposed skin)

Wind Speed	Air Temperature				
	+ 30° F	+ 20° F	+ 10° F	0° F	− 10° F
10 MPH	18° F	4° F	− 9° F	− 21° F	− 33° F
20 MPH	4° F	− 10° F	− 25° F	− 30° F	− 53° F
30 MPH	− 2° F	− 18° F	− 33° F	− 48° F	− 63° F
40 MPH	− 6° F	− 21° F	− 37° F	− 53° F	− 69° F

Rain

Rain doesn't have to be a pain. Generally, only the freezing rains of winter and the driving thunderstorms of summer cause problems, but many walkers will cancel a walk even when it is drizzling. Don't let rain dampen your walking program. As long as you are dressed properly, it is not going to hurt you to go out in a rain shower. Over a T-shirt (or turtleneck if it is cool out), put on a water-repellent nylon jacket that fits loosely enough to allow air to circulate around your body and your skin to breathe. Avoid wearing a plastic slicker; it usually allows no ventilation, and your perspiration will become trapped next to your skin. You will start off very warm, but as soon as you get soaked with sweat, you will get a chill.

One problem with rain gear is that most fabrics that are water-repellent are usually not very breathable, and those that are breathable aren't water-repellent. One fabric, however, called Gore-Tex, is both. Gore-Tex, which was introduced commercially in 1976, is composed of polytetra-fluoroethylene (PTFE) membranes that let vaporized water (perspiration) through but do not allow droplets of water (rain) through. Gore-Tex is used in exercise suits, parkas, tents, and gloves. One drawback to Gore-Tex products, however, is their price—they are quite expensive. You will probably find that you can get by without any particular item.

For people who don't want to be burdened with an umbrella, there are jackets on the market that have a hood with a plastic visor built in to keep rain off your face. If you decide to carry an umbrella, make sure it has a fiberglass or wooden shaft; a metal rod may attract lightning. Wear sturdy, waterproof shoes, since wet feet can cause blisters.

There's no better reason to take a day off than an electrical storm. Lightning is extremely dangerous, killing 125 Americans every year. If you are going out in a spring or summer rain, listen to the radio beforehand to learn whether thunderstorms are expected. If they are, don't go out that day, or at least wait till the storm passes. When you are out in the rain, watch the skies for lightning. If you see a flash, head home or for cover immediately—a car or the inside of a building offers the best protection. If you can't get to either and the storm is upon you, crouch down in a hollow or ditch or, if possible, kneel down on the ground, pressing your knees and feet together, putting your hands on your knees, and bending far forward to make your body as unlike a lightning rod as possible. Whatever you do, stay away from water and out from under trees, and don't touch metal. Be aware, too, that electrical storms are not always accompanied by rain. Heat lightning is common in many areas of the country on warm summer nights.

Darkness

To fit walking into a busy schedule, it is sometimes unavoidable to walk at night—especially in the fall and winter, when it gets dark early. If you do walk at night, walk with someone else. Carry a flashlight, and wear bright-colored clothes, as well as a reflective vest or some other type of reflective clothing (see chapter 11). Walk only on roads or paths you know well so that you do not get lost or hit an unexpected pothole. Make sure you walk facing traffic and only on the sidewalks. (If your area does not have sidewalks, it is best to avoid walking at night altogether, since the risk of getting hit by a passing car is too great.) When cars pass, do not look directly into their headlights. This could temporarily blind you. Look at the ground in front of you so that the bright lights are in your peripheral vision, which is less sensitive to light.

Air Pollution

Air pollution isn't good for anyone, but it imposes a particular health threat to exercisers. When you exercise, you breathe more heavily, taking in larger volumes of air as well as more pollutants. Four types of pollutants pose the most danger to people exercising outdoors: carbon monoxide, oxides of nitrogen, oxides of sulfur, and ozone. Of these, carbon monoxide, found in automobile exhaust and in cigarette smoke, is the biggest problem. This is because hemoglobin, which normally carries oxygen in the blood, will pick up carbon monoxide in the lungs more readily than it will oxygen, thus allowing less oxygen to get to your exercising muscles. Pollution can also harm the delicate tissues lining the airways and lungs. This results in an accumulation of fluid in the lungs and reduces the delivery of oxygen to the blood. All of this makes walking in heavily polluted air especially dangerous for people with emphysema or other lung conditions.

Pollution levels are highest in the summer, when heat, humid air, and sunlight can compound the effects of airborne pollutants. It is important to listen to air-quality reports on newscasts at all times, but particularly in the summer. The Environmental Protection Agency has developed this Pollution Standard Index (PSI) to classify air quality.

PSI Value	Air Quality
0–50	Good
51–100	Moderate
101–200	Unhealthful
201–300	Very unhealthful
301–500	Hazardous

Radio and television stations as well as newspapers in large urban areas regularly report the level of pollution in the area. It is best to cut back on the intensity of your exercise if the PSI value is above 100; do not go outside to exercise at all if the value is over 200.

Here are some other suggestions for easing the unhealthful effects of pollution.

• *Avoid heavily trafficked areas.* Studies have shown that you will inhale more carbon monoxide if you exercise near a highway or a busy street. Walk in a park or a less-congested part of town if you can.

• *Walk before the morning rush hour or after the evening rush hour, when pollution levels are lower.* Air quality is worse in the middle of the day, when it is warmer and the sunlight is stronger.

Hills

When choosing your walking route, you may be tempted to steer clear of hills, but actually hills can be good for you. They can give you more of a workout and can strengthen the quadricep muscles in your thighs. Besides, hills add variety to your route, and in many parts of the country, hills are unavoidable. When you are faced with a hill, don't make a mountain out of it. Just slow down your pace a bit, lean into the incline, take shorter steps, pump your arms hard to help you up, and be comforted by the fact that you get to go down on the way back.

High Altitudes

If you ever walk at high altitudes, you should know that it takes at least a month to become fully acclimated to the thinner air at 5,000 feet above sea level and higher. Until your body adjusts, it is approximately 20 percent harder to do work at high altitudes than at sea level. This is because the air is thinner, and your lungs do not get as much oxygen with each breath. Thus the heart has to beat faster, and you have to breathe faster to make up for the oxygen deficit. So take it easier when you are up in the mountains—at least until your body has adjusted.

Beaches

As you stroll by the sea, there are some specific cautions to keep in mind.

1. Drink even more water than you usually do. The salty environment pulls water from your body, especially if you swim in salt water.

2. Look for hard, wet sand to walk on. Hot, soft sand creates friction and can cause blisters. Soft sand also can cause leg cramps because of the increased stretching and contracting of leg muscles as your heels sink into the sand.

3. Be extra careful to protect yourself from the sun. Sun rays reflect off sand and water, which makes you more vulnerable to burning. Because reflected sun can hit you in spots not normally exposed to the rays, such as under the chin and on the neck and ears, make sure to include these areas when you apply sunscreen.

Threatening People

Tragically, walkers, and other exercisers out by themselves, are sometimes targets for people who are up to no good. Here is what you can do to avoid being a victim on your regular jaunts.

1. Walk with a companion or two, if you can—there is safety in numbers. Do not walk by yourself if you live in a high-crime area or if you are unfamiliar with the territory you will be walking in. If you have a dog, have the animal accompany you on your walks.

2. Walk assertively. "Assertive body language goes a long way in discouraging would-be rapists and [muggers], who choose victims who appear vulnerable or easy to intimidate," says Penny Harrington, the police chief of Portland, Oregon. "You will avoid a great many threats if you stand tall instead of slouching, keep your head up, walk as if you own the street, and, most importantly, make some eye contact."

3. Stay alert. Whether you are walking at night or in broad daylight, be aware of what is happening around you. If you see some dangerous-looking characters in front of you, cross the street.

4. Walk on the side of the sidewalk that has the fewest places for people to hide. Avoid walking by shrubs, dark doorways, and alleys.

5. Avoid isolated areas and walking in the dark. Stick to areas that are fairly well populated. If someone threatens you, walk quickly to a business, a shopping center, or an apartment complex—any place where people congregate. This should deter a potential attacker.

6. Think ahead. If you ever walk through a strange neighborhood, look around carefully to see where you are going and what you must pass to get there. Plan what you would do and where you would go for help if something happened. Look for stores and homes with lights on and for the nearest telephone.

7. React when you first *feel* threatened. If you are walking down the street and sense that someone is following you, turn and ask firmly, "Are you following me?" This shows that you are aware of the person's presence and are not intimidated by it. If the response is no, continue on your way. Your safety is worth the risk of embarrassment. If the person *is* after you, you are in a better position to escape than if the individual attacked you by surprise.

8. Don't carry a purse or wear jewelry. You are only making yourself more vulnerable; besides, a purse will weigh you down and slow down your pace (as well as possibly give you a sore shoulder). If you need to take along money or keys, put them in a pocket or in one of the small packs mentioned in chapter 11.

9. Carry a whistle or a pocket-sized horn or siren (see chapter 11). Loud noises often scare off an attacker and may bring a passerby to your assistance.

Dogs

Dogs may be considered a human's best friend, but often they are a walker's biggest annoyance. Unfriendly dogs can really put a damper on an otherwise pleasant walk. An estimated 3 million dog bites are reported each year, at a cost of about $100 million. Here are some tips from Dr. Michael Fox, the scientific director of the Humane Society of the United States, to help you stay on good terms with the dogs you meet along your route.

1. If you regularly encounter an obnoxious dog, call its owner and ask the person to control it. If the owner does not follow your request, you can lodge a formal complaint with the police.

2. Never stare at a dog. Dogs see this as a threat and may attack.

3. If a dog is barking at you on the edge of its yard, do not abruptly turn and walk quickly away from it. Your sudden flight may arouse its instinct to chase and attack. Instead, walk steadily and slowly, backing away if necessary.

4. If a dog seems exceptionally ferocious, stand your ground and call out to the owner. Hold up a clenched fist and swipe at the animal, shouting in a powerful, angry voice, "No, down! Go home!" This should frighten the dog away.

5. Never lean back if an angry dog is approaching you—it shows that you are scared. Keep your weight forward so that if it jumps at you, you will be ready. If an attack does occur, thrust your knee upward into the dog's chest and strike the dog with your arm.

6. If you are bitten, report it to the police. Your wound, even if it is only a small puncture, should be treated immediately.

(13)

Staying with It

OK, you have taken the big step—you have started a walking program. You have been going out around the neighborhood now for a month or two, and you really feel good about getting your body moving. You should feel good. Starting an exercise program is not easy. Many people drop out in the initial stages, in the first six to eight weeks, before their shoes even get scuffed.

But now that you have gotten started, you face another challenge—staying with it. In order to gain, and keep, all the benefits, walking has to become a long-term, lifelong pastime. Rose Kennedy walked three miles a day until she was ninety, and Henry David Thoreau covered some 250,000 miles during his lifetime. Dedicated walkers like these are able to stick with their programs because they have made walking an important part of their lives—as important, as usual, and as refreshing as a morning shower.

Achieving this dedication is largely a matter of attitude. You should think of your walking program as a change in lifestyle, not merely a change in routine. Lifestyle is long-term; routine, short-term. Fortunately for you, it has been shown that people find it easier to stay with a walking program than with more strenuous exercises. Dr. Fred Stutman, author of *Dietwalk: The Doctor's Fast 3-Day Weight*

Loss and Fitness Plan, found that the dropout rate from high-intensity exercises is more than 75 percent after three to six months. In walking programs, however, more than 75 percent of the participants keep at it.

As you progress in walking, you may go through several stages. There will be the good periods—when you feel terrific, when you can go farther than ever without getting tired, when you can feel yourself getting slimmer and trimmer. But probably there will be times when your walking won't be going as well. The doldrums may hit. This should not surprise you, however. Any long-term commitment inevitably has its ups and downs. By anticipating and knowing how to deal with the downs, you won't let them sink your exercise program.

Boredom

For the most part, boredom is a problem only when you *first* start walking. After six to eight weeks, most people are so attached to their walking regimen that they find it anything but boring. They find it invigorating and relaxing—a time to think, observe, get outside, perhaps talk to a friend.

But there may be times over the years when the thought of a walk makes you yawn for one reason or another. There are several ways to combat this feeling, which is usually only temporary. You may need to change your route. Maybe you have been alternating between two routes near your home for a while, and your boredom comes from seeing the same sights and the same people along the way. A whole new course, away from these other routes, will give you new scenery and, ideally, renewed enthusiasm. If you have been walking alone, get a friend to join you. If you have been walking with a friend or a group, try walking alone for a while. Use a personal stereo if you haven't already, or walk at a different time of day. Variety is the spice of walking.

If these measures do not work, you may be ready to move on to some activity that is a little more challenging, possibly hiking or racewalking (see chapter 14). Or you may want to try jogging, swimming, or biking. You should, however, inform your physician of your intended change to any of these activities. He or she may have some specific cautions.

Frustration

If you walk regularly, before long you should begin to feel and see progress. You should be able to walk farther and faster, and your weight should take a dip. Such encouraging changes can spur you on in your walking program, but, after a while, you may reach a point where your weight or heart rate stabilizes—where you can no longer mark your progress with a new measurement.

Patience must be exercised here—you can't expect to get your body into shape in a few months. (If you try to, you may injure yourself, and that will set back any progress you have made.) Give yourself plenty of time—years, if you have to. And remember that there is just so much weight and so many inches you can lose and only so much you can improve your heart rate. You may have made as much progress as physiologically possible on your present program. In this case, make maintenance of your present physical condition your goal.

However, if you still feel that you would like to improve your cardiovascular system even more, or lose more weight, you may have to go on to a more vigorous exercise program. But again, check with your doctor first. An alternative, as far as weight loss is concerned, is to lower your intake of calories. Once your body gets accustomed to a certain amount of food and a certain amount of activity, you will reach a plateau where you aren't losing weight anymore. You will have to reduce your calories or increase your activity to start losing again.

Whatever you do, don't give up just because you aren't making the progress you think you should. Keep in mind that you will be making better progress than if you stopped altogether.

Time Off

Over the years, there will probably be periods when you have to take time off from your walking—because of illness, injury, personal problems, or maybe because you are in the middle of a crunch at work. If this happens, do not feel guilty. Some things are beyond your control. However, it is important that you get back to your walking as soon as possible.

For every day you take off your walking program, you lose that much conditioning. For example, if you have to take a month off because you are taking care of an ill spouse, when you start back, you will be roughly at the level of conditioning you were at a month before you stopped. Knowing this will help you determine how much you should walk when you begin your program again. So, if you were walking two miles in forty minutes a month earlier, you may be able to pick up again at that level.

However, if you have been sick or injured, you may need to take it even slower, since your illness or injury may have set you back further. Wait until you feel better or until the pain of your injury is gone before starting back, with your doctor's approval.

If you have taken several months or more off and you had been walking with someone else, it is probably not a good idea to start back with your friend right away. He or she may be walking too fast or far for you, and you may push yourself too hard to keep up. It is better to try to get back in shape on your own before joining your friend or to find someone else who is at about the same endurance level.

Be encouraged that your fitness level will probably not sink to that of your prewalking days. You can regain your degree of conditioning in less time than it took to gain it in the first place. You needn't get frustrated and think that all is lost. Begin walking again, buoyed by the knowledge that you have everything to gain by getting back into your program. All is lost only if you quit for good.

Even if you have taken a long hiatus from exercising, restarting your walking regimen will not be as difficult as when you began it. You have the psychological advantage of knowing that you *can* stick with it—that you can leap over the obstacles that stand in the way of a successful exercise program. You have done it before. Keeping this in mind will help you over the hurdles the second time around.

Walking Clubs

One of the best ways to keep your interest and enthusiasm in walking piqued is to join a walking club. The camaraderie and social nature of a club will help make walking more fun. If you want to make exercise an integral part of your life, it is important that you enjoy it.

Walking clubs provide many walking partners and enjoyable walking events, as well as information about health that you may not get otherwise. Many clubs, such as the Fitness Walking Club in Kingsport, Tennessee, invite guest speakers to meetings to let their members in on the latest exercise news.

One interesting event put on by a walking club is a "Match That Time" walk, which is sponsored by the Fitness Walking Club in Kingsport. For this, eight town "celebrities," such as the mayor and city manager, walk a course, and their times are secretly recorded. Later, participants walk the course, and those who come closest to the times of the celebrities win prizes. This club also has a special Christmas covered-dish dinner. Before members eat (they only bring healthy dishes), they take either a two-, three-, or five-mile walk.

A San Diego walking organization called Walkabout International sponsors about a thousand walking events a year. One of its most interesting is a walking tour that takes participants by every ice-cream parlor in nearby La Jolla. The New York Walkers Club sponsors free walking clinics in eight areas around New York City every Saturday morning and such special events as an annual Mother's Day walk. The Walkers Club of America, a racewalking organization with thirty-five chapters across the country, conducts a nine-day camp in the summer exclusively for walkers.

To find out about walking organizations in your area, you can write the Walkers Club of America, 445 East 86th Street, New York, NY 10028. (Please include a stamped, self-addressed business-sized envelope.) The Walkers Club will put you in touch with racewalking organizations, but it still may be worth inquiring even if you do not plan to race. Many members of such clubs do what is called "healthwalking." This is the racewalking form, but without the racing. Even if you do not want to practice the racewalking technique, you may find it enjoyable to be with others who are interested in walking and good health. If you don't have a club near you, why not start one with a few friends and neighbors who also love to walk? The Walkers Club has a kit you can send for that gives you suggestions on how to start a club.

One way to get a group of walkers organized is to talk to a local running club about allowing you to form a branch walking club. This way you will already have a central phone number established and will be able to make use of the running club's resources. In addition, you and other walkers will be able to attend meetings and hear guest speakers. The running club will be gaining a whole new group of members, some of whom may eventually go on to become runners and possible volunteers for its events.

Peet Adams of the Fitness Walking Club suggests that you ask a local hospital or some business interested in good health, such as an insurance firm or a pharmaceutical company, to sponsor a walking club. The Fitness Walking Club is sponsored by the community hospital in Kingsport, Tennessee. The club holds its meetings in the facility, and often doctors from the hospital are guest speakers. Hospital personnel occasionally conduct fitness tests on club members.

To keep up on walking news and to gather ideas on how to keep walking interesting for a lifetime, you may want to subscribe to the quarterly magazine *Walkways*, which is exclusively devoted to walking. A one-year subscription is ten dollars. Write to Walk, Inc., 733 15th Street NW, Suite 427, Washington, DC 20005. The magazine offers health and fitness information, calendars of walking events around the country, profiles of notable walkers, and reviews of books on walking and hiking. In addition, it has features on walking tours of different places around the world.

Starting a walking program is one of the best presents you can give yourself. If you stick with it, it is one that you can enjoy for years to come.

Great Walking Feats

And now for inspiration, here are some of the world's most remarkable walking accomplishments (most are from the *Guiness Book of World Records)*.

• In September 1985, Rob Sweetgall of Newark, Delaware, completed a walk through fifty states in fifty weeks, covering 11,600 miles.

• Dimitru Dan of Romania walked 96,000 kilometers (59,651 miles) over six years (1910–1916) in a contest organized by the Touring Club of France. He averaged 27.24 miles per day.

• Thomas Patrick Benson of Great Britain walked nonstop for 123 hours, 28 minutes between April 11, 1977 and April 16, 1977. He covered 314.33 miles.

• The first person to officially walk around the world was David Kunst of Waseca, Minnesota. He covered 14,500 miles in more than four years, from June 10, 1970 to October 5, 1974. His brother John started off with him, but he was killed by Afghani bandits in 1972.

• Tomas Carlos Pereira of Argentina spent ten years, from April 1968 to April 1978, walking 29,825 miles around all five continents.

• The fastest walk across the United States was recorded by John Lees of Brighton, England, in 1972. He walked 2,876 miles from Los Angeles to New York in 53 days, 12 hours, 15 minutes, which is an average of 53.746 miles per day.

(14)

Advanced Walking

$\mathbf{A}$s you progress in your walking program, there may come a time when you want something a little more challenging to keep your interest in exercise piqued. There are many exercise routes you can take once you get in shape through walking—jogging, biking, and tennis, for example. But you don't have to leave the realm of walking to get a more difficult workout. You could start racewalking—a faster, more regimented version of regular walking—or take up hiking or backpacking. (Although the term *backpacking* is actually defined as "walking with a pack on the back," and *hiking* has no such stipulation, the two terms are often used interchangeably. This is because so many hikers, even if they are going out for the day, carry some gear in a pack with them.)

Here is what you need to know to hike or racewalk safely and enjoyably.

Hiking and Backpacking

The fragrance of fresh pine trees, the taste of water from a cool mountain stream, the sounds of crickets chirping at dusk—these are just a few of the sensory experiences that lure people off the beaten track and into their hiking shoes.

175

"I hike to get out of the city, away from all the people and noise," says Eleanor Townsend, a sixty-three-year-old Manhattan resident who has been hiking nearly every weekend for more than fifteen years. "We all need to get out into the fresh air once in a while. I like to stop and look at the wildflowers." If you want to do some demanding walking and at the same time gain a real sense of adventure, hiking or backpacking may be the ideal activity for you—whether you go on day hikes in the woods nearby or on weekend trips at a national park.

Hiking is a good way to step up the benefits of walking. For example, hiking a rough but level trail expends about 50 percent more energy than the same walk down a paved road. When you go uphill, you increase the number of calories burned dramatically. Walking up a fourteen-degree slope uses up nearly four times as much energy as walking on a level surface. What is more, a 150-pound person hiking at a normal pace for eight hours over varied terrain uses up about 3,500 calories—1,000 more than a good runner expends during a marathon.

If you have never hiked before, you may be somewhat hesitant about venturing out into the "wilderness." You may think backpacking is a sport only for rugged, mountain types. But backpacking is a very individual activity—you pick the place, the distance, and the pace. All it takes is some advanced planning and knowledge to make it less formidable and more fun.

Getting Fit

How do you know when you are physically ready to go hiking or backpacking? Most hiking experts say that you should be able to walk four or five miles comfortably before considering a serious day hike. It is best to begin your backpacking experience with a day hike, not an overnight trip. For an overnight trip, you have to carry more weight, and you should be trail-seasoned beforehand.

Even if you are fit, you will need a little preparation before you leave the smooth, paved roads. Since it is wise to carry some gear with you on a hike, you will need to get used to climbing a slope with extra weight in a pack on your back. Lee Schreiber, an experienced backpacker and author of *Backpacking: A Complete Guide to Why, How, and Where for Hikers and Backpackers,* recommends this pre-conditioning program: Pick a practice route near your home that is about five miles long, with plenty of uphills and downhills. Keep up a brisk pace. Once you feel comfortable with the distance and the terrain, practice with a pack filled with items you will likely be bringing along on a day hike: a sweater, a windbreaker, a small first-aid kit, a lunch, and a plastic bottle of water. Walk your hilly five-mile route with the pack three or four times a week for several weeks. Your goal is to go about five or six miles in two hours. When you can do this, you're ready to hit the trail.

If you are getting ready to go on a long hike, which you should do only after you have successfully completed several day hikes, walk over the hilly route near your home with a heavier pack. This will prepare you for carrying more equipment on a longer trip. Begin with a pack weighing about 5 percent of your body weight. If you weigh 150 pounds, for example, you would carry seven and a half pounds. After you can do that comfortably, gradually add more weight until you can carry 25 percent of your body weight on your back if you are a man, 20 percent if you are a woman. That is thirty-seven and a half pounds for a 150-pound man and thirty pounds for a woman of the same weight. When you can carry this load easily, you are fit to hit the trail for a longer trip.

Where to Go

Before you take off, however, you need to figure out where you are going. Your options are many. Every area of the country is filled with national, state, and local parks that are ideal for hiking. Trail maps are generally available at these parks. Make sure you investigate different areas carefully so that you do not end up on a trail that is too rugged for you. Check to be sure the trails in the various parks are well marked. If you are considering a national park, you can write the National Park Service, the Forest Service, or the Bureau of Land Management for brochures and maps (see page 186). Write to your state tourism board for information about state parks. Other good sources are local and national hiking organizations, your local outdoor shop, a library, or a bookstore. One of the best sources of information and advice is a friend who is an experienced hiker. He or she is probably able to suggest a hiking spot suitable for your fitness level.

Until you become a skilled hiker yourself, it is not wise to go hiking alone. (If you ever do, make sure to leave word of where you are going and how long you will be gone.) Instead, why not ask an experienced friend to take you on a few hikes? Or, failing that, gather a few friends—perhaps some of the people you regularly walk with—and learn together.

One of the best ways to get into hiking is to join a group like the Sierra Club or the Appalachian Mountain Club or a local hiking club. These clubs are perfect for those who want to take the worry out of hiking in the wilderness and do not mind hiking in a group. Your organization plans all the hikes; all you have to do is meet your group at an appointed location and bring your equipment. A group leader will help with any problems you may have and will usually act as a tour guide, pointing out interesting landmarks and vegetation. One caution: Make sure you do not sign up for a hike that is too difficult for you. You do not want to hold the other hikers up because you can't keep up the pace.

Equipment

Proper equipment will make your hike a great deal easier. But before you run out to the sporting goods store and empty the shelves, it is a good idea to stop and assess what you will *really* need. Why spend lots of money on gear you may only use once a year? If you need an expedition sleeping bag at some point, for example, many outdoor shops will allow you to rent one. This saves you from having to buy expensive equipment, and, if you do find you need a certain item, enables you to try out different models before investing.

These are the basics that you should have: sturdy shoes to protect your feet on rugged terrain, a light but sturdy pack to hold your provisions, and clothing that will prepare you for a change in the weather. Following are some suggestions on what to look for in such items. It also helps to find an outdoor shop with a staff whose expertise and advice you trust.

Boots

Not even Colin Fletcher, a longtime backpacking authority who advocates hiking in the buff when possible, would take a step without proper hiking boots. You can get away with skimping on clothes or a pack (though it isn't advisable), but without the right shoes, your feet—and thus you—are going to be miserable. What holds for walking shoes holds true for hiking boots as well: good quality is worth the price. Your feet will thank you for it later.

It used to be that your only choice of hiking footwear was either sneakers or five-pound mountaineering boots. Now, happily, there is more variety. Today's choices range from lightweight nylon shoes that resemble running shoes with thick treads to medium-weight leather boots to very heavy mountaineering boots. Your choice depends on what kind of hiking you will be doing.

For day hikes or short overnights on well-marked trails, you probably do not need shoes weighing more than two pounds. The new nylon hiking shoes are ideal. Many models are reinforced with leather to give extra support in the toe, the middle of the sole, and the heel. They repel water fairly well (but not as well as leather boots) and dry out quickly if they get wet. Jim Chase, equipment editor of *Backpacker* magazine, recommends running-shoe-type hiking boots by such manufacturers as New Balance, Danner Shoe Company, and Vasque. Ask about these brands at your local outdoor shop. The price range for these shoes is between sixty dollars and a hundred dollars.

If, however, you think your hiking may turn into a hard-core hobby, and you will be taking longer hikes, you may want to invest in a more durable pair of leather boots that will protect your feet on rougher terrain. These can weigh from two and a half to four pounds and give your feet more support than the nylon shoes. But if they get wet, they become heavier and take longer to dry than nylon shoes.

Good hiking boots are important if you plan to do more than light walking. Boots come in a variety of styles and weights; the kind of boot you buy will depend on the kind of walking you plan to do—the more strenuous your walking, the more durable and heavy the boot you will need.

Prices on leather boots start around eighty dollars. Among Chase's recommendations in this category are Rockport, Danner Shoe Company, and Merrell.

No matter what boots you choose, the most important thing is that they fit you well. You will be able to break in your boots more easily if they fit properly to begin with. Finding the right boot requires a lot of experimentation; you will probably have to try on a number of different models and sizes before you find what you are looking for. Do not go by size, since your boot size will probably be larger than your normal shoe size and since size varies from one brand to another. Wear the socks you are going to wear on the trail—ideally a thin pair underneath a heavier wool pair—when you go boot shopping.

The boot should fit snugly at the widest part of your foot, it should break at the ball of the foot, and there should be plenty of room for your toes. Test the size by jamming your toes as far forward in the boot as you can. Now try to slide your index finger into the gap between your heel and the shoe. If your finger fits snugly, the fit should be right. If you can place two fingers in the space, your foot is probably going to slide around in the shoe. However, when in doubt, go for the larger size.

Many stores will let you take the boots home and try them out around the house so that you can get a better idea of how they are going to feel in use. Make sure to walk in them indoors only, on carpeted areas, since you cannot return them if they show any signs of wear.

Make sure the boots are well made before you buy them. If the boots are leather, they should be top grain leather. Because seams can eventually break open and tend to leak, the fewer seams the better. Those that the boot has should be sewn with nylon thread and double-stitched at stress points.

In your enthusiasm for your brand-new boots, you may be tempted to take off in them on a hike. But don't forget to break them in first. It will take you very little time to get used to many of the lightweight nylon boots. Leather boots, however, need time to conform to the shape of your feet, and the heavier they are, the more time it will take.

Wear your boots around the house for an hour a day until they feel comfortable. (If they do not begin to feel comfortable after a few days, you may want to exchange them for a different model.) Then progress to wearing them for two or three hours at a time inside. If they still feel comfortable after several days, take them out on your regular walk. Be warned that blisters often accompany the breaking in. (See chapter 9 for information on the prevention and treatment of blisters.) After a week or two, your feet and leather boots should adjust to each other.

Packs

Even if your idea of a hiking adventure is a three-hour ramble through a state park, you probably still will need something to carry your provisions in.

Fanny Pack: This little sack that wraps around your waist is perfect for an afternoon hike. It can hold your lunch, a water thermos, and a rudimentary first-aid kit, which should include, at the least, moleskin for blisters, some bandages, scissors, tweezers, and aspirin or other painkiller.

Day Pack: This is a lightweight sack with adjustable shoulder straps that carries, as the name suggests, enough for the day or a bit more. It is not large enough to use for an extended trip or strong enough for heavy loads. In addition, its construction, which puts all the weight on your shoulders, makes it uncomfortable for carrying big loads.

Weekend Pack: If you ever go on an overnight hike, you will probably want a weekend pack, which has 1,500 to 2,000 cubic inches of space. A pack of this type usually has padded shoulder straps and a waist belt that lessens the amount of pressure on your shoulders by putting more weight on the hips. Some weekend packs have internal frames—rods made of plastic or metal—for more support and to make carrying easier.

Large Pack: Larger, more durable packs with external or internal frames are used on trips of a week or longer. However, it is not worth investing in one unless you go on long hikes regularly. If you need a large pack occasionally, you can rent one from most mountain shops.

Many aches and pains could be avoided with a properly fitted pack. Some shoulder pain when you first get out on the trail is not unusual (even if you have practiced carrying your pack on your regular walks), but generally your shoulders will feel better as they adjust to the load. An aching back is a more serious problem and can indicate that your pack is improperly loaded or that it doesn't fit you properly. A well-fitting pack should conform to your back. If your back does hurt on the trail, Michael Sandi, in his book *Backpacking,* recommends that you occasionally hunch your shoulders and suck in your stomach while you

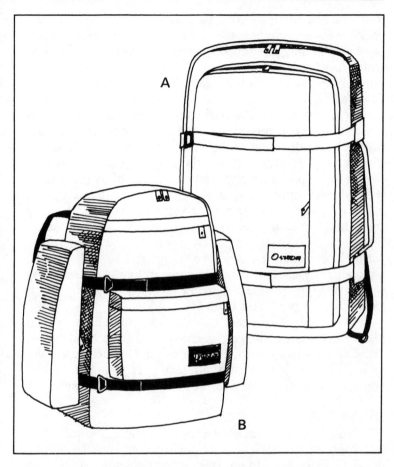

You can carry provisions, rain gear, extra socks, and anything else you need in a day pack. Some packs (A) can be converted to carry-on luggage if you are traveling. The lightweight multipocketed pack (B) chosen by many hikers allows you to organize your load efficiently. Whatever type of pack you choose, make sure it has padded straps to help cushion your body.

push out the small of your back. It also helps to shift the pack's weight every now and then. You can do this by alternately tightening the hip belt while you keep the shoulder straps loose and vice versa.

Clothing

Weather out on the trail can be unpredictable. When you are hiking in mountains or dense woods, the weather can be quite different from what it was at home and can change very quickly during a day's hike. That is why it is best to be prepared for any reasonable possibility (of course, if it is midsummer, you are probably safe to leave your parka at home). Layering is the key when you are dressing for a hike. Wearing several thin layers of clothing means that you can take off or put on a layer as the weather gets warmer or colder. Even in the summer, you will want to pack a light jacket, which may come in handy in the shady woods or high altitudes. A nylon jacket is especially good, since it will protect you from the wind.

Don't forget rain gear. Nothing can put a damper on a hike faster than a shower, unless you are prepared for it. Take along a full-length, fold-up poncho, which can cover your pack too, or a fold-up rain jacket. If you use a jacket, you may need something to protect your pack as well.

On the Trail

Now you are ready to step out into the wilderness—out into fresh air, green fields, and pine-scented forests. But just make sure that you do not step out too quickly. In the middle of such pleasant surroundings, you have to be careful that you do not get carried away and walk faster than you should. If you start out like a hare, you may soon be going slower than a tortoise. Pace yourself, and begin at a slow, steady stride. After a mile or so, increase your momentum as you feel yourself warming up. If you tire and want to stop, do so at short, regular intervals; experts recommend one ten-minute rest stop per hour. If you stop for much longer, you will lose your momentum, as well as the benefits of a constant cardiovascular workout. In addition, your muscles will cool down.

To get the most out of backpacking, you want to conserve enough energy to last you through the day. Walk with
your back straight, your head up, and your shoulders relaxed. Slouching will make you more tired. Step *over* rocks
or other wobbly objects in your path. When the terrain gets
steep, take shorter steps, leaning forward a bit from the
waist to keep the weight of the pack over your feet.

Sandi recommends the "rest step" for really rough going: "Step forward, lean your weight over that foot while
straightening the leg, rest for a second, bring the other foot
forward, lean over it, straighten the leg, rest, and so on."
On downhills, gravity can cause you to bring your feet down
hard, and constant pounding can jar your spine and cause
headache. Try to put your feet down as gently as possible.

To maintain your energy level, you will need plenty of
food and water. Hiking burns up a tremendous number of
calories. A hiker doing even an easy summer hike needs to
take in at least 2,500 calories a day to replace the energy
burned. To make sure your body gets the fuel it needs to
keep it going, eat lots of carbohydrates, which provide more
energy and are more easily digested than most other foods.
Some easy-to-carry foods in this category are apples and
bananas, dried fruits, pasta, and cereals such as oatmeal
and granola.

A common favorite high-energy food is gorp, or trail
mix, which is made of different kinds of nuts mixed with
raisins, coconut, and chocolate pieces. Make sure not to get
too many calories from sugary foods, however. If you do,
your blood-sugar level may actually drop. It is best to supplement sugary foods with something that will provide carbohydrates but is not sweet, such as a baked potato or
whole-grain bread.

Even more important than making sure you have the
right food is making sure you have enough water for your
trip. You should never take even the shortest hike without a
container of water. It is surprisingly easy to become dehydrated, and you usually will not realize it until it is too late.
You normally need a minimum of two quarts of water a
day, but when it is hot out or you are working hard, you
may need twice that amount. Check a map of the area you

plan to be hiking in to make sure you will have sources of water along your route so that you won't have to carry a large amount of water with you. If you do have to bring three or four quarts along on a hike, put the water in three or four separate containers instead of one large bottle. This way the weight can be more evenly distributed in your pack.

You should now have a good idea of the basics of backpacking. But you may want to learn more specifics, such as first aid on the trail and what to expect in high mountain altitudes. Here is a list of information sources that will help get you on your way.

National Park Service, U.S. Department of the Interior, Washington, DC 20240.

Bureau of Land Management, U.S. Department of the Interior, Washington, DC 20240.

Forest Service, U.S. Department of Agriculture, Washington, DC 20250.

The American Hiking Society, 1701 18th Street, NW, Washington, DC 20009.

Sierra Club, 530 Bush Street, San Francisco, CA 94108.

Appalachian Mountain Club, 5 Joy Street, Boston, MA 02108.

Racewalking

If you are not wild about tramping through the wilderness, there is another form of walking you may want to try for a more vigorous workout—racewalking. This is a sport halfway between walking and jogging. On the average, participants walk at 5.5 miles per hour.

But racewalking is more than speedy walking. It involves a very specific technique. A racewalker uses the entire body to propel himself or herself forward in long strides. The feet are planted heel-and-toe, with one foot always staying on the ground and the back leg remaining straight. Although many people think racewalkers wiggle their hips from side to side, they actually rotate their hips forward and downward to gain more speed. During ordinary walking, your body must rise straight over each hip as the corresponding leg swings forward. But by letting your hips rotate, you get around this barrier, and your stride becomes longer and quicker.

At the same time this is going on, a racewalker's arms pump vigorously from waist to chin. Even though some people think that the racewalking form—with the rotating hips and the pumping arms—looks peculiar, the sport is becoming more popular as a safer alternative to jogging and a more challenging alternative to regular walking.

Racewalking first appeared in England in the late nineteenth century. It started as a sport for English gentlemen who competed in long-distance walking competitions. Eventually, walking clubs and associations were formed. The sport made its official entry into the Olympics in London in 1908, which was when the unique characteristics of racewalking were established. According to the British Race Walking Association, racewalking entailed "a long stride, straight knee, toes well up, complete hip action, upright carriage, and vigorous arm swing." In some places, racewalking was called "heel-to-toe."

The sport's form has changed little since then. But in the past decade, people have started racewalking for general fitness as well as for competition. "You don't have to race to racewalk," says Paula Kash, who conducts racewalking clinics in Los Angeles. "You just have to have the correct form." The Walkers Club of America now has about fifteen thousand members, many of whom are in it for their health and to have a good time. Howard Jacobson, executive director, likes to call the sport "healthwalking" to debunk the idea that you have to race.

The major difference between racewalking and regular walking is speed. In addition, says Jacobson, a longtime racewalker who has coached Olympic racewalkers and runs racewalking clinics in the New York City area, racewalking gets the heart rate up much better than brisk walking does. Because the arms are used so vigorously, the upper arms and the pectoral muscles are toned. "In running, my arms go along for the ride. In racewalking, you swing your arms quickly to help propel your legs and the whole body. It helps build your upper body," sixty-five-year-old racewalker Tim Dyas of Ridgewood, New Jersey, says. And he should know.

He has racewalked the New York City Marathon in four hours and fifty minutes.

Racewalking burns off an average of 680 calories per hour; a brisk regular walk at four miles per hour burns off an average of 400 calories in an hour.

Because it is a harder workout, many joggers turn to racewalking—often in preference to regular walking—when they can no longer tolerate the stress that running puts on their knees and ankles. "Racewalkers always have one foot on the ground," says Dr. Thomas De Lauro, academic dean of the New York College of Podiatric Medicine. "This grounded foot supports the body and lessens the jarring impact to the body."

Marie Saunders, a fifty-year-old from Brooklyn, New York, is one of those who left jogging for the relative painlessness of racewalking. "Since jogging felt uncomfortable to me, I chose racewalking as an exercise. I know it's an activity I can take part in until I'm ninety," says Saunders, who took up the sport after cancer therapy. "I really have more energy and feel better since I've started racewalking."

Paula Kash has the same kind of enthusiasm for the sport: "You're very fluid. You're strong; you're flexible. You feel as if you could go on forever," she says.

Getting Started

Since learning the racewalking technique can be a bit tricky at first, you may want to consider joining a racewalking club in your area. Most sponsor clinics where you can learn along with other beginners. Learning how to racewalk properly from the start will help prevent injuries. In addition, racewalking in a group will help you get over the initial feeling that you look silly doing it. "Once you get over the psychological impediment, you're fine," says fifty-four-year-old Bob Bernstein, who walks with a racewalking group in New York City.

If you cannot find a group in your area, talk to the nearest Road Runner's Club (a national running organization with branches in many cities) about starting a racewalking program. Or you can write to the Walkers Club of

America for some how-to information. For three dollars, you can get an overview of racewalking called *Step Lively*. Send your check made out to the Walkers Club of America to 445 East 86th Street, New York, NY 10028. You can also call 1-212-722-WALK for information.

Try to get a friend, or your spouse, to start racewalking with you. It won't be half as hard to begin when someone else is doing it with you.

Warming Up

Going on a racewalk without warming up can lead to muscle tears and injuries, since you will be using parts of your body you may not have exercised in a while. To get your muscles revved up, you should do ten minutes of slow, *easy* stretching, including the warm-up exercises given in chapter 4.

Learning the Racewalking Technique

Start by pointing your toes in the direction of your walk, and reach out with your hip, knee, and heel. Plant your heel on the ground at a forty-degree angle, making sure that the back edge of the heel strikes first. As the edge of your heel hits the ground, tilt your foot slightly so that the outside edge of your shoe hits the ground. This allows a smooth transition from heel to toe. (Rolling on the outside of your foot will prevent your knee from turning inward, which can cause knee problems.) As you walk, each leg performs two separate actions: one is to pull the body forward as the leg swings; the other is to push off from the ground as soon as the other leg has made contact. These two separate motions give racewalkers their speed and power.

Next, put your arms to use, since their swinging motion will help you walk faster, burn off more calories, and tone your upper body. Bend your arms so that the upper arm and forearm meet at a right angle; then pump them rhythmically, in short, pistonlike strokes, synchronizing them with your legs. Your elbows should just skim the body, and your fists should reach shoulder level as they swing up in front. If you are moving fast, your elbows should swing almost parallel to your shoulders in back; at slower speeds, they will

not reach as high. If moving your arms this way feels unnatural at first, just try swinging them loosely at your sides;
then bend them later.

Posture is also important. Keep your head erect, your
shoulders relaxed, and your spine straight. Good posture
also helps you breathe correctly, pulling in that much-
needed oxygen. Remember to breathe deeply, expelling air
while you contract your stomach muscles. This brings air in
efficiently; failure to do so can lead to cramps and side
stitches.

This may seem like a lot to remember, but don't worry
if you don't get the technique down right away. Go slowly in
the beginning until you feel comfortable with the racewalking form. It helps to have a training partner in the beginning
so that you each can make sure the other is racewalking
properly.

How Much to Do

Again, it is wise to resist the urge to do too much too
soon. If you are in fairly good shape (which you most likely
are if you have been participating in regular walking for a
while), try racewalking three times a week on an every-
other-day routine.

A reasonable goal for the first day out would be to
racewalk for about twenty minutes. Assuming you walk
about 90 to 120 steps a minute, you could cover about one
mile in this time. The idea is to increase both your pace and
your distance gradually. As soon as you feel comfortable
with the pace, you might want to increase the time to thirty
minutes and add another workout. Eventually, you want to
be racewalking five or six times a week.

Listen to your body for clues that you are doing too
much. Since you will be using new muscle groups, you can
expect some soreness at first. "The first time I walked with
the local racewalking club, I got sore ankles, and my shins
hurt—I was sore all over. But recently I walked two miles
with the club and had no problem," says Ilene Harrison, a
sixty-seven-year-old racewalker from Yonkers, New York.
If the soreness does not go away, you should slow down a
bit. Ending your workout with proper cool-down exercises

is also crucial for preventing soreness, and this gradually increases your flexibility.

Racing

If you have the competitive spirit, you may want to enter a local racewalking event. Your walking club can plug you into the circuit. The Walkers Club in New York, for example, sponsors grand prix racewalks as well as fun, noncompetitive walks. Look to either your local club or the Walkers Club of America to keep you up-to-date on racing events.

When you enter a racewalking event, however, you have to be concerned about more than your speed. Form is critical as well. Competitive racewalking is one sport, unlike running, in which you can get disqualified if you do not use the proper form. If, for example, you don't straighten the back leg as you proceed, or if the toe of the rear foot leaves the ground before the heel of the front foot strikes, you will be given a warning by a race official. After three warnings for the same offense, you are out of the competition. So, you really do have to know your wiggles and wobbles if you want to start racing.

Appendix
A

Walking is an excellent
activity for strengthening and toning the muscles of your
lower body, especially your legs, but it is not particularly effective when it comes to conditioning the muscles of the upper body. You may want to supplement your walking and
your warm-ups and cool-downs with these exercises for better overall toning. If any of these exercises cause you pain or
discomfort, stop doing them and see your doctor.

Arms, Shoulders, and Chest

1. Stand-up push-ups. Stand a little less than arm's
length from a wall, placing your hands on the wall at chest
height. Lean into the wall, and lower your shoulders and
chest slowly, keeping your back straight and your heels on
the floor. When your chin is close to the wall, push up with
your arms and return to the standing position. Progress until you can do ten to fifteen push-ups.

2. Arm circles. Hold two light books of equal weight,
one in each hand. Start by holding the books at your chest;
then extend your arms out to the sides. Rotate your arms in
small circles, five times forward and five times backward.
Return the books to your chest. Repeat five times.

3. Biceps strengthener. Hold a book in each hand, with your arms by your sides. Bend your arms at the elbows, keeping your elbows at your sides. Bring the books straight up to shoulder level; then lower the books back down to your sides. Repeat ten times.

4. Upper-chest strengthener. Start by raising your arms to shoulder level. Bend your elbows so that your fore-arms and upper arms make a right angle. The palms of your hands should be facing straight ahead. Now bring your arms together slowly in front of you so that the palms of your hands come together and the undersides of your forearms meet. As you bring your arms together, tense the muscles of your chest to offer some natural resistance to the motion. This resistance is what will build strength in your chest muscles. Hold your arms together in front of you for ten seconds; then slowly open them up again. Repeat ten times.

Abdomen

5. Stomach tightener. Sit in a chair with your back straight and your stomach muscles pulled in. Grasp the sides of the chair seat, and slowly raise your right knee while lowering your head. Hold the position for five seconds; then return to the starting position with your back straight against the back of the chair. Repeat five times with each leg, alternating legs.

6. Leg lifts. Sit straight in a chair, with your knees bent and your stomach muscles pulled in. Grasping the sides of the chair, slide your right foot out in front of you on the floor; then raise your leg as high as you can off the floor straight in front of you. Make sure to keep your leg as straight as you can. Then slowly, with control, lower your leg back to the floor. Be careful not to slam your foot to the ground. Slide your foot back to its original position. Repeat five times with each leg, alternating legs.

Appendix
B

MANUFACTURERS

Shoes and Boots

Here is a list of shoe manufacturers and their addresses in case you would like to write for information about walking shoes.

Brooks Shoes Inc.
9341 Courtland Drive NE
Rockford, MI 49351

Brown Shoe Company
8300 Maryland Avenue
St. Louis, MO 63105

California Footwear
3100 Rolison Road
Redwood City, CA 94063

Clarks of England
520 S. Broad Street
Kenneth Square, PA 19348

Converse Inc.
55 Fordham Road
Wilmington, MA 01887

Danner Shoe Company
5188 S.E. International Way
Portland, OR 97222

Dexter Shoe Company
21 St. James Avenue
Boston, MA 02116

Etonic, Inc.
147 Center Street
Brockton, MA 02116

Famolare Inc.
4 E. 54th Street
New York, NY 10022

Laconia Shoes
PO Box 160
Laconia, NH 03246

Maine Woods
19 Bennett Street
West Lynn, MA 01905

Merrell Boot Company
PO Box 1059
Waitsfield, VT 05673

New Balance Athletic Shoe
 Inc.
38 Everett Street
Boston, MA 02135

Nike, Inc.
3900 S.W. Murray Boulevard
Beaverton, OR 97005

Pony Sports & Leisure, Inc.
925 Patterson Plank Road
Secaucus, NJ 07094

Red Wing Shoe Company
419 Bush Street
Red Wing, MN 55066

The Rockport Company
72 Howe Street
Marlboro, MA 01752

San Antonio Shoe, Inc.
101 New Laredo Highway
PO Box 3473
San Antonio, TX 78211

Timberland Company
345 Heritage Avenue
Portsmouth, NH 03801

Turntec
American Sporting Goods,
 Inc./Turntec
1 World Trade Center,
 Suite 8827
New York, NY 10048

Vasque Boots
Red Wing Shoe Company
419 Bush Street
Red Wing, MN 55066

Equipment

Here is a list of some manufacturers of products discussed in chapter 11. You can write to them for information about their products or to find out where the closest retail outlets are that carry their products.

Reflective Clothing and Accessories

Bill Rogers & Company
86 Firrell Drive
Weymouth, MA 02188

Dolphin Activewear
PO Box 98
Shillington, PA 19607

Frank Shorter Sportswear
2400 Central Avenue, Suite I
Boulder, CO 80301

I.E. Sport-Wilco Industries
    U.S.A., Inc.
3820 Del Amo Boulevard,
    Suite 348
Torrance, CA 90503

Insight Reflective Apparel
912 Allepo Street
Newport Beach, CA 92660

Jog-A-Lite, Inc.
PO Box 125
Silver Lake, NH 03875

Joggers D'Lite, Inc.
2500 S.W. 28th Lane
Miami, FL 33131

Kenyon Consumer Products
200 Main Street
Kenyon, RI 02836

M. Nathan, Inc.
920 Broadway Street
New York, NY 10010

Moving Comfort, Inc.
5412 Eisenhower Avenue
Alexandria, VA 22304

National Marker Company
PO Box 1659
Pawtucket, RI 02862

New Balance Company
38 Everett Street
Boston, MA 02135

Sub-4, Inc.
11615 Coley River Circle
Fountain Valley, CA 92708

3-M Company
3M Center, 222–3N
St. Paul, MN 55144

Walking Lights

ATGM Enterprises
2810 Morris Avenue
Union, NJ 07083
(clip-on flashing light)

Trade Source International
PO Box 5158
El Dorado Hills, CA 95630
(lighted vest)

Sound Alarms

Art World Trading Company
32 Gansevoort Street
New York, NY 10014

In-Prop Communications,
    Inc.
12 W. 37th Street, Suite 1211
New York, NY 10018

Personal/Medical Identification Cards

Adventure Sports, Inc.
PO Box 1197
Salt Lake City, UT 84117

Med Card Systems
500 S. 22nd Street, Suite 220
Birmingham, AL 35233

Sacks, Packs, and Pockets

Eastpak
17 Locust Street
Haverhill, MA 01830

I.E. Sport-Wilco Industries
    U.S.A., Inc.
3820 Del Amo Boulevard,
    Suite 348
Torrance, CA 90503

M. Nathan and Company
900 Broadway Street,
    Suite 905
New York, NY 10010

Sports Watches

Accusplit/Timex
2290A Ringwood Avenue
San Jose, California 95131

Casio
300 View Drive
Franklin Lakes, NJ 07417

Cronus Precision Products,
    Inc.
2895 Northwestern Parkway
Santa Clara, CA 95051

Free Style U.S.A.
21025 Osborne Street
Canoga Park, CA 91304

Innovative Time Corporation
6054 Corte Del Cedro
Carlsbad, CA 92008

Seiko Time Corporation
640 Fifth Avenue
New York, NY 10019

Heart Rate Monitors

Accusplit/Timex (see listing
    under Sports Watches)

Amerec Corporation
1776 136th Place NE
PO Box 3825
Bellevue, WA 98009

Baystar, Inc.
110 Painters Mill Road
Owings Mills, MD 21117

Casio (see listing under
    Sports Watches)

Computer Instruments
    Corporation
100 Madison Avenue
Hempstead, NY 11550

Minitech Marketing, Inc.
20710 S. Leapwood Avenue,
    #B
Carson, CA 90746

Pedometers

Accusplit/Timex (see listing
    under Sports Watches)

Cronus Precision Products
(see listing under Sports
Watches)

Precise International
3 Chestnut Street
Suffern, NY 10901

Treadmills

Amerec Corporation (see
listing under Heart Rate
Monitors)

M & R Industries, Inc.
7140 180th Avenue NE
Redmond, WA 98052

Precor USA
9449 151st Avenue NE
Redmond, WA 98052

Roadmaster Corporation
Radio Tower Road
Olney, IL 62450

Sportech, Inc.
401 Euclid Avenue,
Room 141
Cleveland, OH 44114

Trotter Treadmills, Inc.
24 Hopedale Street
Hopedale, MA 01747

Universal Fitness Products
50 Commercial Street
Plainview, NY 11803

Hand and Ankle Weights

AMF American
(Heavyhands)
200 American Avenue
Jefferson, IA 50129

Athletic Fitness Company
PO Box 7191
Auburn, NY 13022-7191

Exerco, Inc.
436 Manville Road
Pleasantville, NY 10570

Fox Marketing
611 N. McLean
Bloomington, IL 61701

I.P.G. Manufacturing
Company
311 E. Elm Street
Reading, MI 49274

Triangle Manufacturing
Corporation
PO Box 30785
Raleigh, NC 27622

MAIL-ORDER HOUSES

Here are the names and addresses of several mail-order houses that carry items that are useful to walkers.

Campmor
810 Route 17 N
PO Box 999
Paramus, NJ 07653-0999

L. L. Bean, Inc.
Freeport, Maine 04033
1-207-865-3111

Mail Runner's Shop
Route 6, Carbondale
    Highway
Scranton, PA 18508
1-800-222-9003

Moss Brown & Company
5210 Eisenhower Avenue
Alexandria, VA 22304
1-800-424-2774

WalkWays Magazine
Woodward Building #426
733 15th Street NW
Washington, DC 20005
1-202-737-9555

References

The following list contains citations for sources quoted in the text as well as selected books, pamphlets, and articles used for research.

Amsterdam, Ezra A., and Holmes, Ann M. *Take Care of Your Heart: The Complete Book of Heart Facts.* New York: Facts on File Publications, 1984.

Bennett, William, and Gurin, Joel. *The Dieter's Dilemma: Eating Less and Weighing More.* New York: Basic Books, 1982.

Blackburn, Henry. "Physical Activity and Coronary Heart Disease: A Brief Update and Population View (Part 1)." *Journal of Cardiac Rehabilitation* 3 (1983): 101–111.

_____. "Physical Activity and Coronary Heart Disease: A Brief Update and Population View (Part 2)." *Journal of Cardiac Rehabilitation* 3 (1983): 171–174.

Blair, Steven N., and others. "Physical Fitness and Incidence of Hypertension in Healthy Normotensive Men and Women." *Journal of the American Medical Association* 252 (1984): 487–490.

Blumenthal, James A., and Williams, Sanders R. "Exercise and Aging: The Use of Physical Exercise in Health Enhancement." *Advances in Research* 6 (1982): 1–5.

Brody, Jane E. "Panel Finds Obesity a Major Killer Needing Top Priority." *New York Times.* February 14, 1985, 1.

Bruce, Robert A. "Exercise, Functional Aerobic Capacity, and Aging—Another Viewpoint." *Medicine and Science in Sports and Exercise* 16 (1984): 8–13.

Cade, Robert, and others. "Effect of Aerobic Exercise Training on Patients with Systemic Arterial Hypertension." *American Journal of Medicine* 77 (1984): 785–790.

Carey, John, and Albow, Keith. "Keeping Fit for Life." *Newsweek,* August 6, 1984, 63–64.

Chobanian, Aram V., and Loviglio, Lorraine. *Boston University Medical Center's Heart Risk Book.* New York: Bantam Books, 1982.

Cooper, Kenneth H. *The Aerobics Program for Total Well-Being.* New York: Bantam Books, 1983.

————. *Running Without Fear.* New York: M. Evans & Co., 1985.

deVries, Herbert A. "Tranquilizer Effect of Exercise: A Critical Review." *The Physician and Sportsmedicine,* November 1981, 47–53.

Duda, Marty. "The Role of Exercise in Managing Diabetes." *The Physician and Sportsmedicine,* September 1985, 164–170.

Eckert, H. M., and Montoyne, H. J., eds. *Exercise and Health.* Champaign, Illinois: Human Kinetics Publishers, 1984.

Fixx, James F. *The Complete Book of Running.* New York: Random House, 1977.

Fletcher, Colin. *The Complete Walker III.* New York: Alfred Knopf, 1984.

Flippin, Royce. "Weight Control." *The Runner,* July 1985, 76–78.

Froelich, Victor F., and Brown, Phyllis. "Exercise and Coronary Heart Disease." *Journal of Cardiac Rehabilitation* 1 (1981): 277–288.

Goodman, Carol E. "Osteoporosis: Protective Measures of Nutrition and Exercise." *Geriatrics* 40 (1985): 59–70.

Greenberg, Herbert M. *Coping with Job Stress.* Englewood Cliffs, New Jersey: Prentice-Hall, 1980.

Gurin, Joel. "Linking Exercise with Longevity." *Runner's World,* April 1985, 62–66.

Gwinup, Grant. "Effect of Exercise Alone on the Weight of Obese Women." *The Archives of Internal Medicine* 135 (1975): 676–680.

Haas, Robert. *Eat to Win.* New York: Rawson Associates, 1984.

Harrington, Penny. "How to Avoid Being a Victim." *McCall's,* September 1985, 98.

Hickler, Roger B. "Nutrition and the Elderly." *American Family Practice* 29 (1984): 137–145.

Holahan, Carole K., and others. "Adjustment in Aging: The Roles of Life Stress, Hassles, and Self-Efficacy." *Health Psychology* 3 (1984): 315–328.

Inman, Verne T., and others. *Human Walking.* Baltimore, Maryland: Waverly Press, 1981.

Jacobson, Howard. *Racewalk to Fitness.* New York: Simon & Schuster, 1980.

Jonas, Steve, and Silver, Nan. "The Last Cure-All." *American Health,* March 1985, 62.

Kannel, William B., and Sorlie, Paul. "Some Health Benefits of Physical Activity." *Archives of Internal Medicine* 139 (1978): 857–861.

Krølner, B., and others. "Physical Exercise as Prophylaxis Against Involutional Vertebral Bone Loss: A Controlled Trial." *Clinical Science* 64 (1983): 541–546.

Leonard, George. "Ultimate Fitness: Life Skills." *Esquire,* May 1984, pp. 149–150.

Londeree, Ben R. "Influence of Age and Other Factors on Maximal Heart Rate." *Journal of Cardiac Rehabilitation* 4 (1984): 44–49.

MacKenzie, Ronald B. "Exercise During the Second Half-Century of Life." *The Corporate Fitness Report* 1 (1981): 39.

Magnus, K., and others. "Walking, Cycling, or Gardening, With or Without Seasonal Interruption, In Relation to Acute Coronary Events. *American Journal of Epidemiology* 110 (1979): 724–731.

Maleskey, Gale. "Don't Be a 'Fall' Guy This Winter." *Prevention,* January 1985, 95–116.

Martin, John E., and Dubbert, Patricia M. "Behavioral Management Strategies for Improving Health and Fitness." *Journal of Cardiac Rehabilitation* 4 (1984): 200–207.

Mazer, Eileen. "All About Angina Relief." *Prevention,* March 1985, 111–120.

Morgan, William P. "Affective Beneficence of Vigorous Physical Activity." *Medicine and Science in Sports and Exercise* 17 (1985): 94–99.

———. "Psychological Effects of Exercise." *Behavioral Medicine Update* 4 (1982): 25–30.

Paffenbarger, Ralph S., and Hale, W. "Work Activity and Coronary Heart Mortality." *New England Journal of Medicine* 292 (1975): 545–550.

Paffenbarger, Ralph S., and others. "A Natural History of Athleticism and Cardiovascular Health." *Journal of the American Medical Association* 252 (1984): 491–495.

Port, Steven, and others. "Effect of Age on the Response of the Left Ventricular Ejection Fraction to Exercise." *New England Journal of Medicine* 303 (1980): 1133–1137.

Richter, Erick A., and others. "Diabetes and Exercise." *American Journal of Medicine* 70 (1981): 201–207.

Sagalyn, Arnold. "The Pace of Business." *WalkWays,* Winter 1985, 11.

Sager, Kayleen. "Senior Fitness—For the Health of It." *The Physician and Sportsmedicine,* October 1983, 31–36.

Sandi, Michael. *Sports Illustrated Backpacking.* New York: Harper & Row, 1980.

Schleifer, Steven J., and others. "Suppression of Lymphocyte Stimulation Following Bereavement." *Journal of the American Medical Association* 250 (1983): 374–377.

Schreiber, Lee. *Backpacking: A Complete Guide to Why, How, and Where for Hikers and Backpackers.* New York: Stein & Day, 1983.

Schwartz, Leonard. *Heavyhands.* New York: Warner Books, 1984.

"Sex and Exercise." *Vogue,* June 1985, 114.

Shapiro, Colin, and others. "Fitness Facilitates Sleep." *European Journal of Applied Physiology* 53 (1984): 1–4.

Shea, Timothy P., and Smith, Joan K. *The Over Easy Foot Care Book*. Washington, D.C.: AARP; Glenview, Ill.: Scott, Foresman & Co. 1984. (An AARP Book)

Sheehan, George. *Running and Being: The Total Experience*. New York: Simon & Schuster, 1978.

Shellock, Frank G. "Physiological Benefits of Warm-Up." *The Physician and Sportsmedicine*, October 1983, 134–138.

Shephard, Roy J. "The Value of Exercise in Ischemic Heart Disease: A Cumulative Analysis." *Journal of Cardiac Rehabilitation* 3 (1983): 294–298.

_____. "Motivation: The Key to Fitness Compliance." *The Physician and Sportsmedicine*, July 1985, 88–101.

Shepherd, Jack. "Ultimate Fitness: Aerobics." *Esquire,* May 1984, 92–94.

Silver, Nan. "How to Eat More and Weigh Less." *American Health,* March 1985, 110–116.

Simon, Harvey B. "The Immunology of Exercise." *Journal of the American Medical Association* 252 (1984): 2735–2738.

Smith, Everett L. "Exercise for Prevention of Osteoporosis: A Review." *The Physician and Sportsmedicine,* March 1982, 72–79.

Smith, Everett L., and Gilligan, Catherine. "Physical Activity Prescription for the Older Adult." *The Physician and Sportsmedicine,* August 1983, 91–101.

Solomon, Henry A. *The Exercise Myth*. New York: Harcourt Brace Jovanovich, 1984.

Stamford, Bryant. "Why Do Your Muscles Get Sore?" *The Physician and Sportsmedicine,* November 1984, 147.

_____. "Exercise and Longevity." *The Physician and Sportsmedicine,* June 1984, 209.

Stark, Elizabeth. "Exercising Away Depression." *Psychology Today,* December 1984, 68.

Stifler, John. "Walking: Get Hip." *The Runner,* September 1985, 28.

_____. "The Hand Weights Debate." *The Runner,* July 1985, 21.

Stutman, Fred A. *Dietwalk: The Doctor's Fast and Easy 3-Day Superdiet and Fitness Plan.* Philadelphia: Medical Manor Books, 1984.

Thomas, Marguerite. "Heal It With Walking." *Prevention,* June 1985, 90–95.

Tyne, Philip J., and Mitchell, Matt. *Total Stretching.* Chicago: Contemporary Books, 1983.

Walking for Exercise and Pleasure. Washington, D.C.: The President's Council on Physical Fitness and Sports, n.d.

Wallis, Claudia. "Stress: Can We Cope?" *Time,* June 6, 1983, 48–54.

————. "Hold the Eggs and the Butter." *Time,* March 26, 1984, 56–63.

Weltman, Arthur, and Stamford, Bryant. "Exercising Safely in Winter." *The Physician and Sportsmedicine,* January 1982, 130.

————. "Safe and Effective Weight Loss." *The Physician and Sportsmedicine,* April 1982, 141.

————. "Designing a Safe, Sound Exercise Program." *The Physician and Sportsmedicine,* July 1982, 177.

————. "Exercise and the Cigarette Smoker." *The Physician and Sportsmedicine,* December 1982, 153.

————. "Beware When Exercising in the Heat." *The Physician and Sportsmedicine,* May 1983, 171.

Williams, R. Sanders, and others. "Guidelines for Unsupervised Exercise in Patients with Ischemic Heart Disease." *Journal of Cardiac Rehabilitation* 1 (1981): 213–219.

Wood, Peter D., and Haskell, William L. "The Effect of Exercise on Plasma High Density Lipoproteins." *Lipids* 14 (1979): 417–427.

————. "California Diet and Exercise Program." *Runner's World,* June 1983, 36.

Yagoda, Ben. "Ultimate Fitness: Relaxation." *Esquire,* May 1984, 125–128.

Index

About the Author

Jeannie Ralston is a contributing editor to *McCall's* magazine and frequently writes about health and fitness. She has worked for two newspapers, the *St. Petersburg Times* and the *Kingsport Times-News;* has written for *Venture, Sport, Health, Seventeen, SatGuide, Satellite Orbit,* and *Carolina Lifestyles;* and is coauthor of the book *My Life as a Robot* (Congdon & Weed, 1984). Ms. Ralston is a graduate of the University of South Carolina School of Journalism and is originally from Kingsport, Tennessee. She currently resides in New York City.